COUNTRY TALK AGAIN

ILLUSTRATED BY VAL BIRO, FSIA

COUNTRY TALK AGAIN

J. H. B. Peel

ROBERT HALE · LONDON

© J. H. B. Peel 1977

First published in Great Britain 1977

ISBN 0 7091 6371 1

Robert Hale Limited
Clerkenwell House
Clerkenwell Green
London EC1R oHT

Printed in Great Britain by
Willmer Brothers Limited, Birkenhead

Contents

It is by learning to cherish our own little tree, or field, or brook that we become fitted for a wider and deeper affection.

R. S. Thomas

I

An Englishman's Home

By way of what the Irishman called a winter spring-cleaning I
lately sifted an accumulation of old papers and photographs. The
sifting, of course, had its painful aspects, for no one enjoys digging
his own grave. Nevertheless, a man who refuses to bury the past
will soon find himself interred beneath it, or at any rate so
besieged by it that his attics and shelves create a kind of claustrophobic wall.

Among the papers which I did *not* destroy was a pink-ribboned
document wherewith the lawyers conveyed to me this house and
certain small fields around it. The conveyance was something
more than a certificate or proof of ownership. It was a medieval
reminder that all land is held of the Crown, and that the Crown
alone may lawfully grant ownership of land. William the Con-
queror kept a close watch on the licensing of landlords. Except
along the Scottish and Welsh borders, where defence was para-
mount, he reduced the risk of rebellion by rationing the area of
land and with it the degree of authority which any one subject
might hold in any one locality. Her present Majesty, however,
needs not feel uneasy about the extent of my own estate. Were I
to raise a rebellion. a single policeman would quell it. Even so,
the pink-ribboned document stated my name and the extent of land
conveyed to me via the previous owner thereof. Neither Bracton
nor Selden could have devised a stronger proof of proprietorship.
If he wished to dispute my own rights, a squatter would need to
stand up . . . or so I had assumed, until I noticed a mouse entering
from the garden with all the assurance of an owner-occupier.

Some moments later, while setting a trap outside the door, I observed that several birds were roosting in my trees and under the rafters of my wood shed. They evidently regarded the property as their own insofar as their ancestors had enjoyed use of it for many centuries. Then a worm appeared, as if to assert that the document contained a clause granting him the right to dig for minerals. I soon began to wonder whether the laws of property ought not to be strengthened with a *caveat homo*.

Wandering through one of the paddocks, I saw a rabbit disappearing in the general direction of Australia; and when I dug a toecap in the soil, I uncovered a colony of ants unashamedly at home. None of this was a threat to my rights, but it did emphasise the difference between ownership and possession, because if the latter really does constitute nine-tenths of the former, then the birds and the insects and the animals regard my pink ribbon as no more binding than Brother Michael Foot's assurance that we shall not be forced to join a trade union. On reflection, however, I welcomed the non-paying guests, provided always that I remained free to eject such squatters as slugs and greenflies.

While watching the coming and going of creatures for whom mine was a Garden of Eden, I wondered idly whether the sight of their nest or the scent of their burrow aroused in them the affection which stirs in me whenever I see the house from afar, sited skilfully near the brow of a hill. That anthropomorphic question posed another ... the same, in fact, which puzzled Hamlet: do the spirits of the dead return to haunt their earthly habitat? Reason (whatever that may be) cries: "Never!" But intuition (another mysterious entity) whispers: "Who knows?" Perhaps a well-beloved house really does attract the ghosts of those who once lived there, even as it attracted Hardy's returning native:

> Back to my native place
> Bent upon returning ...
> To be where my race
> Were well known ...

What, then, of the men who built this house three centuries ago, unaware that their two cottages would one day be joined together in stony matrimony? Had I the eyes to read between the lines of the conveyance, would I discover that to my own proprietorship were added those of John Brown, Chas. Davy, Thos. Cobleigh, Jos. Pennyfold, and others of a rustic company whose names no man may number? Whether ghostly or not, those long-departed families had left their mark on the place . . . rusty nails from which they slung kettles, blackened hearths in which they burned logs, stone walls dividing paddocks, flower beds embalming beauty, footpaths *en route* to the well and the lane and the wood. Did I overhear a Victorian shepherd criticising my handiwork? "They were a tidy little pair o' bedrooms afore he ripped 'em open and stacked a whole heap o' books round the walls. What's he want books for, anyway? I never had no use for 'em. 'Twas all I could do to write 'Jos. Pennyfold' on my marriage lines." Jos. himself, however, was not utterly blinkered by his inability to read and write, for he belonged to the breed whom Gilbert White classified as "stationary men," and the roots of such rustics delve deep; not, indeed, to Australia nor even to London, yet far enough to discover where the badgers are, and why the brook failed, and how the parson died, and what the butler saw.

Perhaps, after all, Hamlet did over-estimate the quantity of things which philosophy cannot perceive. Perhaps Jos. Pennyfold and Thos. Cobleigh and Chas. Davy and John Brown do *not* go marching on, not even to haunt their old homes. Perhaps All Hallows' Eve is an April Fools' Night. Yet one thing remains certain; if your house has been inhabited since the Stuarts reigned, you will sometimes think of the occupants who were Jacobites under the Hanoverians. You will think of those who lost a son at Trafalgar, and received back a father from Inkerman. You will mourn their bereavements, and rejoice at their baptisms, and attend their weddings. And while leaning on a gate, gazing fondly at the hills, you will become aware of your own place in the procession.

The Hour Before Dawn

It was dark and very cold. Ice blurred the bedroom windowpane. Downstairs a bellows fanned last night's embers in the kitchen hearth. Suddenly the dry twigs flared, scenting the curtained room. The farmer's wife—known to her family as Mam—served cups of tea, hot and sweet. The farmer himself wore khaki breeches, a flannel shirt, a tattered cardigan, and carpet slippers over grey stockings. Like many other Welshmen, he might have passed for a Spaniard. Time had not frosted his black hair; only the grey stubble dated him.

Mam began to prepare the breakfast that would greet us when we returned at seven o'clock. "Ifor," she warned, "don't be late, man. It's my day for Maison Maisie. Dewi is fetching me eight o'clock sharp."

Ifor meanwhile had stepped into his gumboots, and was priming a hurricane lamp. "Okay," he said to me. "Let's go."

An icy dagger thrust itself through the open doorway, striking first the face, then the fingers, and finally the spine. "Watch out," Ifor exclaimed. "It's slippery." It was indeed, for mud had over-sealed the yard. There was no moon, no stars; only blackness, and wind roaring round the mountain, and bitter cold. The shippon, too, was cold, but less bitter than the yard. Three cows blinked at the hurricane lamp as we entered. A cat looked up from the straw, yawned, and went to sleep again.

Ifor's task was to feed the turkeys; mine, to slice roots for the herd. We lit a second lamp, and slung it from a nail on one of the cobwebbed rafters. Ifor's bucket clattered across the stone floor while our stooping bodies flipped hunchback shadows over whitewashed walls.

"Damn that wind!" Ifor growled. A gust had ripped open the upper half of the door, swaying the lanterns, raising the chaff, bristling the cat. Ifor went outside, bucket in one hand, lantern in the other; and presently, above the wind, I heard the gobble-gobble of greedy turkeys.

The root slicer, being seventy years old, had seen many innovations, from tractors and book-keeping to insecticides and insolvency; yet its first owner—Ifor's father—bequeathed the shippon in much the same state as he inherited it from his own father. He, too, had kindled a fire at six o'clock, and lit the lantern, and crossed the yard, and sometimes glanced eastward, seeking the first streak of dawn.

Having sliced the roots, I shovelled them into a heap beside the door, ready for the trailer that would carry them to pastures near the cwm. That done, I went in search of my host, whom I had first met several years previously, when his house sheltered me from what would otherwise have been a bleak night on a bare mountain. I found him in a linhay beyond the brook, tending his cob.

"It is cold," he muttered. "Or else I am growing old. I never used to feel the cold. In fact, I . . . but there it is. No good looking back. That's what Da always said. 'Keep going, boy,' was his motto. Well, I've done that all right. It's seven years since Mam and me took a holiday. And even then we only went to Bangor. Ah, and it rained. I rubbed my hands, though. 'Mam,' I told her, 'another day like this and maybe we shall cut some hay after all.' But she only looked at her sunshade and said, 'It's as well I brought my umbrella.' "

He ran his fingers through the cob's mane. "My grandson," he mused, "was seventeen last month. He sweeps the floor in a factory at Birmingham, working five days a week, if you can call it work, with dinner vouchers and a paid holiday. That kid earns more than I do, though I work seven days a week, and take no holiday at all, and cook my own dinner whenever Mam visits the hairdresser." He examined his cracked fingernails. "Why do I do it, eh?" Then he glanced up, as though it was I who had asked the question. "For love, not for money. It is in the blood, you see . . . in Da's blood and way back to my great-grandfather of the Ebenezer Chapel. And before that?" Again he answered his own question. "Drovers we were, taking cattle and sheep over the mountains to London. Ah, and down from Scotland sometimes."

He patted the cob, unhooked the lantern, and led the way outside, casting a yellow glow on waterlogged ruts, ruffled hens, swirling straws, quivering branches. The darkness seemed eternal. Had dawn died? Ifor peered eastward in search of an answer. "We shan't see it yet awhile," he decided. "Too cloudy. But it is there, mind, and will be when we're not." Somewhere a cock crowed. "We'd better get home to breakfast, else we'll have Maison Maisie ringing up about the perm."

We trudged through the mire, over the planked brook, past the shippon, into the yard, following a routine which Ifor had observed for half a century. In the kitchen we removed our gumboots, rinsed our hands, and then sat down expectantly. Mam had everything ready; a blazing fire, gallons of tea, haunches of bacon, wedges of fried bread, and six poached eggs like suns on a white sky. Ifor said a grace in Welsh, and the echo of his Amen almost coincided with the first mouthful.

After breakfast Mam pointed to a saucepan beside the stove. "Put it on at eleven o'clock," she reminded us, "and give it a couple of hours. Now I must feed the hens." She wrapped a shawl over her head, and stood for a moment in the open doorway. Once again the icy dagger rushed in, but the doorway itself was no longer a black rectangle. Vague shapes could be seen in the yard . . . a tree, a plough, a corner of the shippon. As Ifor had remarked, dawn lives longer than men, and is more punctual.

Love Songs and Roses

Long before Freud issued his imprimatur, men had acknowledged the role of Eros by assuming that a love song was a sex song. Freud himself, of course, assumed that all songs are sex songs, not least the sacred songs wherewith we sublimate or render respectable our erotic instincts. Well, it may be so. I cannot say. Even Jung had his doubts. The point is, we still do assume that all love songs are sex songs, the sort of things which brought fame to Catullus and the late Ivor Novello. But what about William Cowper's love song?

England, with all thy faults, I love thee still.

Granted that Cowper was psychotic. Granted, if you must, that every Englishman either consciously or unconsciously regards England as his Motherland, or Mistressland, or the Land which —for a multitude of recondite reasons—he chose to espouse as a creature more predictable and less dangerous than women. Granted those things, Cowper's *confessio amantis* was nevertheless addressed to a place, not to a person. It evokes visions of thatched roofs and green hills and wooded valleys. It does not—or I hope it does not—evoke visions of film stars and Miss World. If, therefore, we allow that patriotism or love of a country must include love of a countryside, then the man who believes that his own region cannot be sufficiently praised, or has never praised at all, needs only consult the poets in order to find himself refuted. Consider Essex, that flat region, long since colonised by London, Colchester, and an eczema of intermediate eyesores. Even in

Essex some beauty has survived. How much more beautiful the county must have been when Edward Thomas strung its place-names into a necklace:

> If I should ever by chance grow rich,
> I'll buy Codham, Cockridden, and Childerditch,
> Roses, Pyrgo, and Lapwater,
> And let them all to my elder daughter.

Cambridgeshire is another countryside seldom to be found in the travel brochures, yet when Rupert Brooke sipped lager in Berlin he was seized with a sudden yearning for flat fields and an east wind:

> would I were
> In Grantchester, in Grantchester!

Sussex has been swamped with praise by Kipling and Belloc, neither of whom was a native of the county. Wilfred Scawen Blunt, on the other hand, was a Sussex squire born-and-bred; and after a lifetime's wandering he returned *con amore* to his ancestral seat near Southwater:

> Dear checker woods, the Sussex Weald!

Sailing home from America, John Masefield paced a midnight deck, eager to reach his homeland:

> Into a darkness now I stare
> Towards where Wrekin lifts in air
> And Severn glides ...

On the other side of the Welsh border, W. H. Davies remembered the days "when poetry first began to warm my blood." And ever after, he felt partly an exile:

> Ah, when I see a leafy village now,
> I sigh and ask it for Llantarnam's green ...

From Scotland came the voice of Sir Walter himself:

> Land of the mountain and the flood,
> Land of my sires!

Michael Drayton paid a grateful compliment to Warwickshire:

> My native County, then, which so brave spirits hast bred ...

B

T. E. Brown exhorted his fellow-Manxmen to defend their island:

> Dear countrymen, what'er is left to us
> Of ancient heritage,
> Of manners, speech, of humours, polity . . .

John Drinkwater etched the Cotswolds:

> I see the wagons move along the rows
> Of ripe and summer-breathing clover flower,
> I see the lissom husbandman who knows
> Deep in his heart the beauty of his power . . .

The litany is almost as old as English poetry. William Langland sang of Worcestershire; William Browne, of Devonshire; John Clare, of Northamptonshire; George Crabbe, of Suffolk; Emily Brontë, of Yorkshire; Tennyson, of Lincolnshire; William Barnes, of Dorset; Swinburne, of Northumberland; Mary Webb, of Shropshire; Siegfried Sassoon, of Kent; George Meredith, of Surrey; Robert Bridges, of Berkshire; John Masefield, of Herefordshire. Prose, too, in its other harmony, has uttered a regional thanksgiving. Gilbert White spoke for Hampshire; Charles Lamb, for Hertfordshire; Richard Jefferies, for Wiltshire; Rider Haggard, for Norfolk; Charles Reade, for Oxfordshire; Arnold Bennett, for Staffordshire; D. H. Lawrence, for Nottinghamshire; S. L. Bensusan, for Essex; Beatrix Potter, for Lancashire; Quiller-Couch, for Cornwall. Sometimes the praise is confined to a relatively small area: Eden Phillpotts, for instance, evoking Dartmoor, and R. D. Blackmore, distilling Exmoor.

Literary criticism and topographical preference are in the last resort matters of taste, and we all know—or used to know— what the Romans thought about *that*. Yet we may still ask an unrhetorical question: has any county ever received from its sons a blessing more beautiful than that which Wordsworth bestowed on Westmorland and Cumberland?

> Dear native regions, whereso'er shall close
> My mortal course, there shall I think on you.

Blizzard

At dawn the wind abated, but not the cold. At noon the clouds formed a single sheet, grey and very low. At three o'clock, in premature darkness, snow seemed imminent. Ten minutes later it arrived, flouncing like feathers from a sky so still that the flakes fell in straight lines, covering all things equally. Even while

you watched, tussocks of grass turned white. At one moment the world was apparently unpeopled; at the next, life bustled in every cottage and farm. Housewives appeared, snatching linen from the clothes line, cradling logs in the porch, dragging perambulators to the shed. Firelit windows reflected John Clare's wintry scene:

> While snows the window panes bedim
> The fire curls up a sunny charm
> Where creaming o'er the pitcher's rim
> The flowering ale is set to warm.

Children stared up at the sky, and one of them held out the palm of her hand, as though the flakes were manna from heaven. Footsteps changed from a clop to a crunch, sounding the same on gravel as on grass. An infinite universe contracted into a claustrophobic continuum which excluded both the sky and the skyline, substituting instead a damp and whitewashed wall.

At four o'clock a car's headlights shone from the moor, then halted and went back, the motorist having decided that reversal was the better part of discretion, for snow would soon obliterate the landmarks. All sounds were muffled, and some scarcely audible. But keen ears could detect the snow as it struck the leaves of a holly bush with repeated soft blows that created a rustle. At six o'clock the hayricks wore a white thatch, nearly as tall as a chef's cap. Then a breeze stirred, and became a wind and finally a gale which, instead of scattering the clouds, called-up reinforcements, hurling the blizzard against walls, windows, and whatever else stood in its way. There were no dainty snowflakes now, no graceful curtsies. The charming ballet had become a menacing reality, stinging the eye, sealing the lashes, thrusting a cold hand through collars and cuffs.

In mountainous country the natives are accustomed to snow. When it does arrive they take certain precautions, often by telephone. "Gran?" says a voice. "It's Florrie speaking. Is Dad still there? Well, just tell 'en to get cracking. Why? The snow, of course. Lord bless us, midear, don't 'ee never look out o' the window?" Some people allow a neighbour to pave the way. "Idris here. Cwm Fawr. You'll soon be having a tractor coming up, I shouldn't wonder. You will? In that case, I'll risk taking the car." At remote crofts in the Scottish Highlands, where the snowscape may be several weeks old, even the rent collector comes as a pleasant surprise. "Why, it's Fergus Macmoneybags. Sit ye doon, mon. We've no' seen a soul since Thairsday."

The snow is drifting now, blocking lanes at an angle of forty-five degrees. Signposts on the high moor sink from sight while cattle wander in search of shelter, and the red deer re-enact Edward Thomas's nightpiece:

> Out in the dark over the snow
> The fallow fawn invisible go
> With the fallow doe;
> And the winds blow
> Fast as the stars are slow.

Meanwhile, unheard above the gale, three telephone wires snap, leaving their strands to sway like frisky pendula. As though mimicking a jingle-bell sleigh ride, the postman's van clinks its chains, for the Royal Mail comes and goes regardless of the weather. Twice already the postman has lent his shovel to a motorist whose rear wheels skidded into a drift. Suddenly the gloom is gashed by vivid gleams from a snowplough worming its way uphill. "Just my luck," the driver tells his mate. "Bingo night and a bloody blizzard." He points to a cottage at the far end of a blocked track. "While we'm yere we may as well give access to Grannie Newton. The poor soul's been on her own since Tom died." The driver makes a brief detour. A door opens, shuts, re-opens after five minutes, and back churns the plough. "Game old girl is Grannie. Ah, and her makes a good cup o' tea, too. If only . . . 'old 'ard, mate! Another wire down." The driver peers ahead. "And yere's some madman taking a midnight stroll."

Waist-high in drifts, an oilskinned youth looms out of the whiteness.

"Are you lost," shouts the driver, "or just loony?"

"Neither," comes the reply. "I'm on my way to see how Mrs Newton's doing."

"Her's doing fine. Radio full-blast, a fire halfway up the chimney, tea all round, and a bottle o' ginger wine to keep the witches away. But 'twas a kindly thought, all the same." He quizzes the sou'-westered face. "Are you Joe Davey's boy?"

"That's me."

"I thought as much. I can recognise a Davey nose afore ever it opens its mouth. Hop on board, and we'll take 'ee as far as the crossroads." The plough lurches forward again. "Old Joe's soon going to have to do some digging."

"We'm digging already," the youth replies. "Some o' the ewes was six foot deep. And the ponies don't like it neither. Still, we'm used to it up yere."

Already the snow has thinned the tyremarks, and a wind carries away the voices. Soon the red lamps disappear in a white void. No one is out of doors who can sit beside the fire. But the birds and certain other wild creatures are less fortunate. Although feather and fur may protect them against the cold, only chance or a compassionate cottager will supply their breakfast.

2

Candlemas

Town life holds no monopoly of change. Even the remotest hamlet is a kaleidoscope. Every day—or so it seems—the farmer meets a new vaccine, a new spray, a new insecticide. Ancient houses give way to modern. The dead are buried, and the infants are baptised. Crop rotation alters the look of the land while erosion changes the shape, adding an inch to one place, subtracting a foot from another. Motorways race where lanes once ambled, and factories bury cornfields. In that sense, therefore, a chronicler of the rural scene must be an evangelist, perpetually announcing some new thing, though not always a good one.

"The earth," cried the Psalmist, "abideth forever." Wiser in our generation, we know that nothing abideth forever. There was a time when the English Channel did not exist, and a time when Lyonesse did exist. Nevertheless, man's threescore-years-and-ten perceive no change in the basic behaviour of the sky, the sea, the seasons; nor have the centuries wrought much difference. The Mercians who built Offa's Dyke heard a thrush in February, and waited eagerly on the year's first snowdrop, and hoped that the spring would prove less boisterous than its predecessor. In short, the seasons exert a profound influence on countryfolk, and it is quite wrong to suppose that such people take those things for granted. At about this time of year an old Welshwoman will say: "Beautiful the snowdrops on Mynd Gwyneth. It does my heart good to see them." A leathery-faced gamekeeper, walking the Durham moors, will report: "T'owd wren is nesting in't gurt elum tree." A taciturn Scottish ghillie will spread the good news by asking a question: "Did ye no' see the wee crocus on yon brae?" Shepherds, too, are steeped in the silence that accompanies solitude. They seldom use three words where one will suffice, and never a word at all when gestures speak for themselves. Yet shepherds count the small calendars which point the way to spring ... the catkins, daffodils, anemones, beech buds. G. M. Trevelyan went to the root of the matter when he said:

"The face of our living mother, the Earth, has a language that appeals to the deepest in us. 'Unworded things and old' stir unremembered racial memories ..." On that point at least, the Freudians and the Jungians are agreed.

Some people, of course, feel genuinely surprised that anyone should pay much attention to daffodils or snowdrops. Flowers, they believe, are mere toys, whereas politics and economics are real life. For all we know, even the Stone Age may have begat men whose chief aim in life was to increase "productivity" by devising a more "efficient" method of flint-knapping. Nature, by contrast, is in less of a hurry to "develop" herself. The February lanes and fields are lined with punctual yet leisurely calendars which catch a country eye. If the weather is mild, a potentilla opens its white flower, and the first anemone appears, confirming that its Greek name, *anemos*, means "wind," and that the frail plant does not fear a buffeting. In the far south-west a few primroses may have bloomed; even, perhaps, the earliest Lent lilies. Among winter's brown bracken the sweet violets shine like particles of purple plush. Tight as a rolled umbrella the green spikes of cuckoo-pint obtrude. Already the kingcups or marsh marigolds are in bud, soon to pave the streams with gold. Woods show the dark leaves of dog's mercury, and the rising bluebells make another milestone on the road to May.

In February the foxes go vixening. Squirrels, too, have mated. You can see their nest-like drays slung astride the bare branches. Much scuffling is heard when a squirrel raids his own larders . . . larders in the plural, you notice, because squirrels bury their food in more than one place. Amid all the change, therefore, a country-man observes the same old events recurring in approximately the same old way at the same old time; and it is pleasant to know that the back streets of grim towns share something of the renaissance when parks and gardens offer their quorum of birds and their quota of colour. Countrymen are not the only ones who hear the calendar unfolding. Wherever two or three trees are gathered together, there a thrush may utter Meredith's springlike song:

> His Island voice you then shall hear,
> Nor ever after separate
> From such a twilight of the year
> Advancing to a vernal gate.

But was anyone ever satisfied with February? Winter, after all, is the most exacting of the seasons and the least varied. The meadows look much as they did four months ago. The trees have scarcely altered since a November gale stripped the last leaf from the final bough. The temperature may be lower, and the wind keener, than on Christmas Eve. Our eyes ache for a blue sky. Our bones crave the south wind. Our life begins to wish itself away. Unlike T. S. Eliot, most countryfolk believe that the cruellest month is February, not April. There indeed lies the rub, that our hunger for the main dish may cause us to despise a nourishing aperitif. Spring at its best is all very fine, but to hibernate between October and February is to squander one-third of a short span. The utmost concession we should grant ourselves is a restrained impatience when winter at last shows signs of spring. If the impatience becomes irritable we lose our grip on what Aquinas called *Nunc fluens* or the omnipresent Now. In culinary terms these brusque days of February ought to be sampled willingly. J. C. Trewin offers the right recipe for enjoying the year's menu:

> My winter is my spring:
> No fleeting seasons hurry by,
> No cheating time can bring
> Red rust upon the ivy frond,
> Bare boughs upon the tree.

A Countryman Born and Bred

He lives on his brother's estate, and the villagers call him "Mr Edward." As a younger son, he has been a feature of country life ever since primogeniture was practised in England. It is true, of course, that many younger sons either went into commerce or entered one of the three ancient professions, yet there has always been a residue who lived where they were born. When Addison depicted a landless scion in Will Wimble, he regretted that the amiable rustic had not become a businessman: "What good to his Country or himself," he asked, "might not a Trader or Merchant have done with such useful tho' ordinary Qualifications?"

Mr Edward himself could never have endured the sedentary routine of office life. Modest to the verge of diffidence, he knows that his sole claim on the world's attention is his plight as a quasi-dodo, dwelling in a corner of his paternal acres, some of which have been sold in order to pay death duties and the next generation's school fees. Chroniclers of the contemporary scene are familiar with Mr Edward's attitude to the destruction of family estates: "It saddens me, of course, but I see no point in going on about it. Spilt milk and all that. Or stolen milk. It depends on whether you happened to own the cow. Anyway, the clever ones will manage to salvage something from the Socialists. You can be damned certain the Socialists will." Mr Edward, at all events, was born forty years ago; and the ensuing decade convinced both himself and his parents that the event had been an anti-climax, for whereas the heir did brilliantly at Cambridge, and is now doing well enough to subsist on his remaining acres, poor Mr Edward achieved nothing more spectacular than a lovable disposition. While the elder son combined chemistry with classics, the younger fished his father's streams; and when the elder added estate management to his expertise, the younger merely learned to care for ailing animals.

Mr Edward lives alone in what used to be the headkeeper's cottage, which stands on the edge of Merryfield Wood. His brother did equip the place with a small generator, but Mr Edward prefers the quietude of lamplight and the fellowship of firelight. "All the same," he explains, "I switch the refrigerator on during summer, just to keep the butter from boiling." Both within and without, the cottage is as spick and span, partly because the occupier is by nature a tidy person, and partly because a woman from the village comes each day to cook a meal and to wield a duster.

Is Mr Edward a handsome man? Young women think not, though the older ones allow that in thirty years' time his strong-boned features will be as ruddy as they are now, and his six-feet as supple and as slim. On most days he might be mistaken for the headkeeper's ghost because he often carries a gun, and usually wears breeches. Long hours in wind and rain have so rasped his complexion that summer merely deepens a perennial tan. His income is fifteen pounds weekly, that being as much as the heir can afford to pay in return for services as an unnecessary bailiff. By way of perquisites, Mr Edward receives free board and lodging, free hunting, free maintenance of a 1932 Alvis, and the loan of his brother's second-best dinner jacket for the Hunt Ball and other formal soirées.

Three things about Mr Edward help to form a first and lasting impression. They are his self-acceptance, his love of the country-side, and his happiness. "I can honestly say," he confessed, "that I've envied only one person in my life, and he was Jack the poacher. You never saw any man handle a snare like old Jack could." This unselfishness extends to the estate which he did not inherit. Indeed, he admits that providence was wise when it granted precedence to his brother: "Tony knows all about income tax and the latest broiler houses. Somehow or other he'll keep the flag flying. But I never could have demolished our Tudor barn and put-up that Dutch one. Whenever I see the damned thing it kills any desire I may have felt to visit Holland."

Although his love of the countryside could hardly be deeper, it might grow wider if he could be persuaded to forsake his own countryside. As it is, he confines his travels to an annual week of deer-stalking in Scotland and an occasional weekend of fly-fishing in Hampshire. Yet, as his brother keeps pointing out: "Why don't you accept more often? They'd all love to have you as their guest."

And his happiness? That was an inheritance, more precious than money. From it and into it flows his self-acceptance as a creature whose intellectual attainments are slight, whose cultural tastes are narrow, whose personal ambitions scarcely exist. "Politics?" he will say. "Why, yes, they're very important. Of course they are. But they don't happen to be my own line of country. I vote for what I believe are the right people, and I try to do what I believe are the right things. It's as simple as that. Besides, there's always something going on here, even in winter, even at mid-night ... which reminds me ... did you know those badgers have come back?"

Not, then, a brilliant man; some will say, an ineffectual man. Beyond doubt he is an unfashionable one. Fabians steal his patrimony, Freudians probe his celibacy, and fools dismiss him as a figment of sentimental imagination. Yet those who know him value him. They enjoy the quiet homeliness of his cottage. They are able to relax in his company, to rest from the task of asserting their own superiority, for no one bothers to impress a man who feels no need to impress others. Above all, they admire his knowledge of local people and places and animals. If they wish to identify a pawmark in the snow, or a strange bird-call at dawn, they consult Mr Edward. It is he who tells them where the springs break soonest, why the Luddites spared Merryfield Farm, when the mill last earned its daily bread, and how the crossroads came to be called Queen's Corner.

The Ideal Walking Companion

Walking sticks are less common than they used to be, chiefly because walking is less common. Some people, indeed, never carry a stick, and would regard one as a hindrance. To others a good stick seems almost as important as stout shoes. Robbed of its support, such people feel as lost as a huntsman without his spurs. Leigh Hunt equated a walking stick with the walker: "Deprive a man of his stick, who is accustomed to carry one, and with what diminished sense of vigour and gracefulness he issues out of his house. Wanting a stick, he wants himself."

The best walker I ever knew would as soon carry a stick as a handbag. I once tried to convert him, but without success. He began by shifting the stick from one arm to the other, rather like a drum-major. Then he tucked it under his elbow; then he slung it over his shoulder; and when at last he did use it as a means of propulsion, his limbs lost their ability to co-ordinate, as though he were a recruit learning to march. Having twice tripped over the thing, he entangled it with a drain, and was visibly relieved when it snapped in half.

Umbrellas are not as a rule carried by countrymen, who would rather get wet than be seen sheltering under a portable tent. History, however, shows that several eminent pedestrians either carried an umbrella or used it in lieu of a stick. Wordsworth, for example, composed poetry while pacing the garden at Dove Cottage; and when the rain fell he paced under an umbrella. His contemporary, Canon Hutton, walked from Warwickshire to Northumberland and thence along Hadrian's Wall, armed with an umbrella. "I fastened with a strap," he wrote, "an umbrella in a green case, for I was not likely to have six weeks' tour without wet . . ." Hutton cannot fairly be called a milksop, because he made the journey during his eighty-second year. George Borrow as a bachelor walked in Bohemian attire with his belongings tied in a bundle; but when he married a naval officer's widow he assumed the mantle of gentility, which included black clothes

and an umbrella. In *Wild Wales* he cited the merits of that umbrella, not only as a poignard against brigands and bulls but also
as a mark of quality when entering an inn or meeting a stranger.

In theory, almost any timber will serve to make a walking
stick. In practice, however, few people choose elm, poplar,
birch or elder. E. V. Lucas favoured something fruitful: "I have,"
he boasted, "carried my present cherry for a good five years."
F. R. Higgins sang a song to his faithful sloe:

> So armed as one, have we not shared each journey
> On noiseless path or road of stone;
> O exiled brother of the flowering sloe tree,
> Your past ways are my own.

Myself, I prefer ash, a light yet strong companion. In youth it
wears a grey bloom; in age, a subdued gloss, deepened by mud
and some honourable scars. Beware the stick with a curved handle,
for the curve was imposed artificially, and will begin to uncurl
after a few months. Handles should form a right angle with the
rest of the stick, and the angle itself should result from natural
growth. On short walks there is much to be said for sticks with a
knobbly handle, about the size of a pullet's egg, which fits like a
castor in the palm of the hand. At the other extreme comes the
blackthorn, a self-defensive companion, much favoured in the
years when criminals carried cudgels. My own blackthorn weighs
nearly three pounds, and could crack the thickest skull. It is
indeed a stick, descended etymologically from the Old Teutonic
stik, meaning "to pierce".

Shops ply a brisk trade in thumbsticks or tall staves, which
nowadays fetch upward of one pound fifty, though they flourish
like weeds in any copse, and as timber are worth a few pence per
score. Edward Thomas would have rejected such mass-produced
reach-me-downs. According to Eleanor Farjeon, "he would rather
be seen dead than walking with a stick he hadn't cut for himself.
Going along a hedge, his eye never missed a straight limb of hazel
or holly or thorn or ash standing up from the root that would
plant itself in his palm as the perfect handle . . ." Thomas's widow
gave Eleanor Farjeon one of his favourite sticks, "a warm-
coloured hazel, with down-tilted crutch . . ."

A real walking stick is neither a gimmick nor an ornament. It
is a servant that has become a friend, quick to assist while des-

cending a slippery hill, or defying a frightened cow, or pioneering a passage through brambles. In short, it assumes the role of a walker's *alter ego*. Like a suit of clothes, the ideal walking stick must be made-to-measure. Half an inch may make all the difference between compromise and perfection. Weight, too, is important. No true walking-sticker would climb Helvellyn with the cane which he carries when strolling to the postbox. If you cannot make a stick, you should seek one of the country craftsmen who cut the sticks they sell, like the master-sticker at Hawkridge on Exmoor. Three minutes' sampling will discover the ash that fits, or can be re-shaped to fit, your own needs.

As smokers choose a pipe to please their mood, so walkers choose a stick to span their journey. To possess only one stick is like having only one book, or one shirt, or less than two socks. For short distances it is best to carry a stick that can be twiddled; for anything over six miles you will require a gnarled and nostalgic veteran; a stick that has heard the chimes at midnight echoing through a snowfilled wood; a stick that has supported your chin while you watched a May Day dawning; a stick that has retrieved a cap from a cliff, that has chastised unfriendly cattle, and basked beside inn fires, and hacked fairways among overgrown footpaths; a stick worthy to be preserved as a faithful fellow-traveller who, when your own walk is at last confined to the garden, will summon up remembrance of what Robert Bridges called "the long lighthearted days that are no more."

Pastoral Symphony

We met by appointment near the edge of the moor. The shepherd arrived on his own pony. I came by courtesy of Shanks's. It was a sunny day—blue above and green all around—with thrushes singing, lambs bleating, and rooks raucously renovating their nests. "A week of rain," the shepherd admitted, "might have spoiled everything. Cold we can cope with, but a damp lamb is halfway to being a dead one."

The ewes were pedigree Exmoors, sometimes called Porlock moorland sheep, a horned and hardy breed, descended from the old English mountain flocks. They can nibble a living at nearly

two thousand feet above the sea. Down in the combes the low-land Suffolks had lambed on New Year's Eve, but the Exmoors waited until February, protected against rain by straw pens which served as an emergency ward for any ailing lamb. The shepherd meanwhile eyed his flock, counting them more quickly than a computer. "Three missing." He stood up in the stirrups, peering above a ridge of high ground. Then he uttered several whoops, rather like a destroyer coming alongside, and away bounded one of his three dogs. Before I had climbed the ridge, the vagrants were rounded up and returned to base. Meanwhile, the shepherd quizzed a lonely-looking lamb. "The ewe won't take to 'en," he explained. "It does sometimes happen." He lifted the waif. "'Tis the bottle for 'ee, milad. Or a foster if we can coax one."

"The others seem well enough," I remarked.

"For once in a while the weather's on our side. If they'd lambed earlier this month some of 'em would have been washed away by the floods."

Things have changed since W. H. Hudson wrote his memoir of a Wiltshire shepherd's life eighty years ago, when lambing meant days of solitude in a hut on the downs. It was at just such a hut that Bathsheba Everdene first met Gabriel Oak, the hero of *Far From the Madding Crowd*. Hardy described the hut as "a small Noah's Ark . . . on little wheels which raised it a foot above the ground. Such shepherd's huts are dragged into the fields when the lambing season comes on, to shelter the shepherd in his enforced nightly attendance." A modern shepherd seldom keeps watch over his flock by night. Telephones and cars allow him to sleep peacefully and, in a crisis, to arrive quickly.

Not many years ago I met a Northumbrian who as a child had watched the annual hiring fair in Wooler, at a time when elderly shepherds still wore smocks, and carried the crooks by which a farmer recognised their calling. Having bargained for a year's employment, master and man sealed their unwritten contract with ale in lieu of God's penny or a deposit on account. Some shepherds continue to receive a rent-free cottage, the right to buy old hurdles as firewood, and gifts of grain and clothing. A similar bargain was struck in 1642, when Sir Henry Best, a Yorkshire squire, engaged Simon Hewson to tend two hundred and fifty sheep at an annual wage of four pounds plus "6 sheep, his howse rent, and two bushels of oats besides one shilling godspenny."

C

Few young people nowadays have ever heard a sheep's bell, but during my own childhood some of the flocks in deep country tinkled a bucolic carillon. The bells, however, were not devised in order to charm the ears of melodious farmfolk. They performed a useful service by helping the shepherd to identify his flock from a distance and to retrieve any stragglers. As music, the sound was delightful. It brought Arcady to England, varying with the size of the bells and with the movement of the ringers. I last heard it—much to my astonishment—in 1961 when three ewes rang three tunes from a hilltop paddock beside a thatched cottage overlooking Bledlow Ridge in Buckinghamshire.

A shepherd holds an especial place in the affections of country-folk, for his calling is a symbol of loving-kindness, the Good Shepherd; and although modern transport has eased his duties, it has not yet impaired his skills. There are times when—having trudged to the top of a mountain—he must diagnose and, if possible, cure a sick animal. During an emergency his only instruments may be a penknife and hurricane lamp. I have known many shepherds. None of them died before he was seventy; several are alive and alert at eighty; and each agreed that he would gladly do it all over again. Such men speak from the heart. "I did truly love my sheep. They'm not over-intelligent, mind, but they'm purty smart when it comes to obeying a dog. They'm dear things, once you've learned their ways. And every one of 'em looks different. Some people say that shepherding was a lonely life, but I never found it so. I'd the birds to watch, and the rabbits to bait, and all manner o' clouds and rainbows and sunsets. And at night I'd the moon and the stars, and a stove burning in the hut, and alongside me a dog, the truest creatures God ever made. I can remember all their names, even after sixty years.

"Mind 'ee, 'twasn't a soft life, but what man wants to be soft? Nowadays they'm all for saying how bad everything was. Well, I leave that sort o' talk to folks with a big mouth and a little brain. Most of 'em don't know what they *are* talking about, 'cause in them years their parents wasn't born. In the end it amounts to this . . . a shepherd brings food and fleece to such as need them. He sees the land as God made 'en, afore certain folks took to development and the like. He learns things that are worth knowing, even though they'm not written in books. He's up with the sun, and if he's lucky he's in bed soon after midnight. But he

enjoys life, and when the times comes he'll go easy. Isn't that
better than slaving your days at a job you despise in a place you
detest?

"Feed my sheep, says the Bible. Well, I've done that all right.
In fact, I once overdid it, and Lord how that farmer cussed, even
though he *was* a lay preacher."

Britain on the Rocks

Hadrian, you remember, caused a wall to be built; and so did I.
But there the likeness ends, for whereas Hadrian's Wall was built
by thousands of soldiers, my wall was built with my own two
hands. Like Hadrian's, however, the wall has won some praise—
all five feet of it—and is to me a source of self-commendation,
the more so because I am by choice an unpractical person, at any
rate when tinkering with recalcitrant machinery. On reflection,
I ought perhaps to confess that the work was rather a reconstruc-
tion than a creation *ab initio*. In other words, part of the wall had
collapsed, and after two halfhearted attempts at clearing the
stones, I did at last follow King Harry's example: "Once more
into the breach, dear friends . . ."

In theory, anybody can build a wall; you merely set one stone
on another; but in practice the craft offers a variety of expertise.
My own method was simple. Having assembled the materials, I
chose those stones that were most pleasing to the eye and best
suited to the angle. That done, I commenced the jigsaw, taking
care to pack the pieces with soil and some tufts of grass. The
result would not appear impeccable to the Capsticks of Westmorland, who—father and son—are champion stonewallers; yet the
breach has been mended, and the mending is blending.

Job, we are told, had no answer when God said to him: "Where
wast thou when I laid the foundations of the earth?" In Job's
day and for many centuries thereafter those foundations were
regarded as uniformly solid and comparatively cool. Later
generations discovered that the bowels of the earth regurgitate
molten larva and inflammable liquid. Nevertheless, the human
race is in a sense founded on rock, so that any survey of rural life
remains shallow until it delves below the surface. Rocks, after

all, affect our crafts, customs, clothes, food, industries. Every countryman's library ought therefore to contain a geological map, the only sure guide to Scott's architectural skyscape:

> The rocky summits, split and rent,
> Formed turret, dome, or battlement,
> Or seemed fantastically set
> With cupola or minaret.

The medieval Cotswold masons did not build in stone simply because they preferred it to wood; nor did the men of the Sussex Weald build in wood simply because they preferred it to stone. They used the materials that were plentiful and at hand. Likewise the Chiltern folk used flint from their chalk hills; East Anglians used reed thatch from their Broads and meres; Welshmen used slate from their mountains. Earthquakes and climate decreed that Cornwall should breed tinners; that Devon should breed sailors; that Nottinghamshire should breed colliers. Salmon—a staple diet in Perthshire—was at one time a rarity in Rutland. The Scots ate porridge because oats is the only cereal that can withstand a high altitude and poor soil.

Rocks can often be identified via the objects on their surface . . . the sandstone churches of Herefordshire, the Suffolk sugar beet, Kentish coalfields, Caithness peat bogs, Surrey pine trees, Dorset marble. Erosion and climate made Lancashire a county of cotton and clogs; and for the same reason the Fensmen became wildfowlers, the Northumbrians became sheep farmers, the Severnsiders became fishermen, the East Anglians became flint-knappers, the Middlesexers became market gardeners, and the Lord Chancellor sat on a woolsack. These differences exist not only within each county but also within a single garden, as, for example, when the flower beds reveal a rift of clay. Some rocks are confined to a very small area, like the serpentine stone in the Lizard Peninsula.

As with technology, so with geology: Britain led the field. The *très magi* of the science were born during the eighteenth century. First came William Smith of Churchill in Oxfordshire, a roadmender who studied the rocks and then produced the first geological map of England and Wales, basing it on his discovery that fossils can help to estimate the age of rock strata. Second came Adam Sedgwick, son of the vicar of Dent in Yorkshire.

Educated at the village grammar school (which is still endowed though now defunct), Sedgwick proceeded to Sedburgh School and thence to Cambridge, where he became Professor of Geology. He has two memorials at Dent; one in the parish church, the other (a slab of granite) in the cobbled street. Third came Roderick Impey Murchison, a Ross-shire man, who, having served at the Battle of Corunna, resigned his commission in order to study the rocks. Murchison and Sedgwick put the English language on the geological map. Thus, Sedgwick chose the name "Cambrian" for the oldest Palaeozoic rocks because he had first studied them in Wales, which the seventeenth-century antiquaries called Cambria. Murchison, for his part, gave the name Silurian to a later period, the Silures being a Welsh tribe. On some topics the two men differed with academic acrimony. Thus, while Sedgwick classified certain rocks as Upper Cambrian, Murchison declared that they ought to be classified as Lower Silurian. In 1879, when both of the disputants were dead, Professor Lapworth of Birmingham University classified those rocks by their present name, Ordovician, after the Ordovices, the last Welsh tribe that surrendered to Rome.

Geology throughout the world now bears an English nomenclature: Cambrian, Ordovician, Silurian, Devonian. The term Permian recalls the researches which the Tsar invited Murchison to make in the Province of Permia; and the terms Pliocene and Eocene recall the Greek scholarship of Sir Charles Lyell. If this planet is destined to suffer catastrophic upheavals, and if men survive those ordeals, then the rocks may still be described in English words, even although Cambria became a lake, and Devon sank alongside Lyonesse.

3

Putting the Clock Forward

Everyone would rather put the clock forward than back. This so-called Daylight Saving—first conceived by Benjamin Franklin —was not practised until the early years of the twentieth century, when a Chelsea builder, William Willett, campaigned for its introduction. In 1916 the Summertime Act of Britain was passed, chiefly in order to save fuel and lighting. It is true, of course, that the "extra hour" may coincide with a fog or with a blizzard; true also that the hour is not at all an extra, but can be obtained simply by adjusting one's daily routine to that of the sun. Nevertheless, the ritual is something more than a custom; it is a legal injunction, and those who ignore it will find themselves out of time with current events. More, then, than a custom —more, indeed, than an injunction—the extra hour is a confirmation and an affirmation, for it announces that the sap is surging, that the buds are swelling, that the temperature is rising, and that the weekenders are saying "Yes" to Cecil Day Lewis's question:

> Can you not hear the entrance of a new theme?
> You who go out alone, on tandem or on pillion,
> Down arterial roads in April . . .

March is the month when country talk tells a new time of year. You meet it first in the mild south-west when a housewife complains: "This sunshine makes the curtains look as if they'd been hung over a bonfire." In Ireland the Reverence's sister exclaims: "Faith, if we don't soon turn the place inside-out we'll all be upside-down." From Wales comes the same cry: "There's soot for you! Next winter we either go all-electric or you buy me a gas mask." Scotland, too, echoes the domestic dismay: "Dinna' bother to ask where flies go in the wintertime. Just take a peep behind yon bookcase."

In deep country the annual spring cleaning retains much of its ancient ardour. Every moveable object is moved. Mats and carpets and curtains are slung over a clothes line, there to receive a resonant spanking. Buckets of soapy water are slopped onto stone floors. Head-averted mothers slam books open-and-shut while tiptoeing daughters thrust broomsticks into cobwebbed crevices. Menfolk, on the other hand, solicit mutual sympathy at the Red Lion. "I've been turned out of my own house, bach. The missus is at it again. Even taken the newspapers from under the linoleum. Next thing, she'll be dusting the bloody dustbin!"

A passing stranger might suppose that some of the cottages and their contents are being auctioned. Tables and chairs litter the lawn. Coal scuttles, pictures, and mats line the path. It is not unknown for a brass bedstead to be dismantled *in situ* and then lowered piecemeal from an upper window. At the back door a wash tub bubbles over with curtains, chair covers, and other household drapes. Bribed with helpings of jam tart, a small boy polishes dad's medals, grandad's horse brasses, and sundry *objets d'art* (acquired from Japan via Blackpool). Many of those mass-produced articles are so hideous that they would have horrified an eighteenth-century country craftsman. Occasionally, however, you will see a gate-legged table whose value now exceeds five years' wages of the man who made it.

Houses are not the sole beneficiaries of spring cleaning. The land itself wears a new look. Walk down any country lane during late March, and you will notice that winter's withered stems are falling away. Every fern grows green. The grassblades glint, and above them the daffodils and primroses are in flower. On plough-land in chalk country fresh-turned furrows wink whenever a sunbeam catches the flints. Birds build nests, soon to be camouflaged among young leaves. Day by day the volume of the dawn chorus increases. Down by the sea, blue-jerseyed fishermen and peak-capped yachtsmen look to their nets or to their sails, making and mending with the nimbleness of milliners. Ropes hang from rusty nails on seaweed jetties while oilskins mime headless scarecrows alongside lobster pots that resemble filleted buoys. Clifftop farmhouses extend a terse invitation: *Vacancies*. At quayside hotels the deck chairs spring up like premature mushrooms. Wearing sun glasses for Eastertide—and probably a raincoat as well—the heirs of Nelson gaze spellbound and mystified while a fisherman's eight-year-old son propels his praam with a flick of the wrist on a single oar. And when at last the extra hour begins to fade, a yachtsman returns from the year's maiden voyage, a harbinger of halcyon days and calm nights.

In some ways the arrival of official summertime can seem quite dramatic, especially if the weather takes a sudden change for the better. On a stormy evening, when the ploughman enters the Wheatsheaf for a pre-supper pint, the lights are on, and the logs in the hearth have been burning all day. In the porch he doffs the sodden sack that has shielded him against the hail. Next evening, having put his clock forward one hour, the ploughman arrives in sunshine. No lights are on, and the tap room fire is only five minutes old. After supper, instead of watching television, he works in his garden, murmuring an immemorial commonplace: "The days are drawing out, eh?"

Although it may come in like a lion, March must be received as a lamb, otherwise the winter seems interminable, and spring itself an interlude that ended before it got under way. Come rain, come shine, the mythical extra hour acts like a tonic, for men crave the light, and are fearful of the dark. Frost or fog, somebody somewhere mows the lawn at six o'clock in the evening; somebody digs the soil at seven o'clock; and at eight o'clock somebody answers: "Just coming. One more barrowful and I've finished."

Since no one knows what really did happen, we may as well believe the Bible: "and darkness was upon the face of the deep . . . and God said, let there be light: and there was light."

A Village Romance

Mr Chips, the retired schoolmaster, was baptised Charles Edward Algernon Morville-Crecy. His widowed sister, who keeps house for him, is Mrs de Montfort-Jones, known informally as Miss Chips. On Easter Sunday she puzzled the villagers by announcing that she would soon cease to be either a Miss or a Mrs. When the penny had dropped, the news spread. "'Tis as I've said all along. Miss Chips is to marry Sir Richard, and they'll both live at the Hall."

Women do ultimately reach an age at which the probability of marriage becomes improbable, but men are never so old that a conspiracy of matchmakers ceases to regard them as eligible. Mr Chips being hale and still in his sixties, the village ladies consider him as overdue for matrimony. Sometimes, indeed, they try to hasten his arrival there. Thus, the district nurse, who once bandaged his thumb, became greatly excited when another of her patients mentioned that a Greek widow, Mrs Katastropholis, lived only nine miles away. Mr Chips, the nurse reasoned, was a Greek scholar; therefore he liked Greek; therefore he liked Greeks. Alas, Mrs Katastropholis proved to be an African trapeze artiste who had married her late employer, a professional lion tamer. Hope revived, however, when the doctor's daughter learned that Glebe Cottage was about to be acquired by a middle aged spinster, Miss Nun. But hope dwindled when further investigation revealed that, despite her name, Miss Nun was by no means vowed to chastity. The colonel's wife then suggested that her own sister-in-law might (as she put it) do very well. But once again a fatal flaw appeared, for whereas Mr Chips is a confirmed agnostic, the sister-in-law turned out to be a fervent follower of Zen. Fully aware of the plot, Mr Chips took the colonel aside. "Conceivably," he allowed, "one might co-habit with a Roman Catholic, because there *is* such a thing as a lapsed Papist, but whoever heard of a non-practising Buddhist?"

Then came the day when all those machinations were overshadowed by the news that Miss Chips was indeed engaged to marry Sir Richard, a robust widower. Conducted by the bridegroom's brother, a bishop, the wedding took place in the parish church. And what a wedding! Never before had the village witnessed such a gathering of the County. The deputy lord-lieutenant was there; two former high sheriffs; a pewful of peers; and one admiral in the organ loft (he had arrived late, and was misdirected by an usher). The bride really did look radiant, like a second spring shining with autumnal serenity. In place of a florist's bouquet, she carried a posy of spring flowers that had been picked before breakfast by the village schoolmistress and three of the senior girls. Mr Chips himself, having spent the previous day in minor skirmishes with moths, appeared impressively coat-tailed, looking more than ever like Sir Edward Elgar. The best man was the bridegroom's eldest son, of whom the bride's domestic "help" remarked: "He's an officer in the Domestic Cavalry. They guard the Queen, and you mustn't feed them while they're on duty." All hearts went out to the cavalry-man's son, aged six, who paced the aisle with the precision of a predestined page, accompanied by his sister, aged four, who was visibly delighted with her new pink shoes, which she offered for inspection by the congregation.

More than two hundred guests attended a reception at the Hall, including sixty villagers who either worked on Sir Richard's estate or were otherwise employed in the district. Among those who toasted the happy couple was a tramp who, having mingled with the crowd at the lodge gates, smuggled himself into the succulent atmosphere of salmon and cigar smoke. After the fifth pint he removed the silver teaspoons from his pocket, and replaced them with cigarettes ... an act of self-denial which rewarded itself when the tramp was spotted and searched by the baker, who had shut up shop in order to don his uniform as a special constable. But all feuds were forgotten in the general rejoicing. Even the sharpest hatchet buried her axe. A Socialist councillor did mutter something about hungry miners, but fell silent when the blacksmith suggested that the cost of the councillor's new car (the second in three years) would feed several families for several months.

After the reception the couple drove away to a secret destination, which the sexton believed was "probably the Costa Bravura." The postmistress, on the other hand, said she had good reason to believe that the honeymoon would be spent at Sheringham, where Sir Richard owned a house overlooking the sea. Meanwhile, festivities at the Hall continued long after the bride and bridegroom had departed. At six o'clock the page and his sister declared that they ought not to go to bed until seven o'clock. When they did go, at half-past eight, the bridesmaid refused to remove her pink shoes. At nine o'clock a belated dinner was served to the handful of relatives and close friends. At eleven o'clock the bishop and the best man were still playing billiards. At midnight the last guest departed. At one o'clock in the morning, however, a group of estate workers emerged unsteadily from the kitchen, but found difficulty in proceeding beyond the kennels. After three unsuccessful attempts to reach the drive, they bedded down with Sir Richard's pack of beagles.

And Mr Chips? Did he return to a lonely home, bereft of his sisterly housekeeper? He did indeed, but not indefinitely, because he, too, will reside at the Hall, in a suite above the stables. Sir Richard, in fact, has had the stable clock repaired so that its sonorous voice will remind Mr Chips of the years when from his rooms in New College he heard the chimes at midnight, scholarly chimes, speeding his notes on "A Definition of the Platonic Idea." So, another chapter of local history has closed, to be continued at the Hall and to last, one hopes, for many happy years.

Getting to Know the District

How long does it take a newcomer to feel at home in a strange countryside? The answer depends partly on age. A young man, setting-up house for the first time, will adapt himself quickly, whereas an elderly man, whose previous house had been his home for half a century, will be slow to settle, and can never settle deeply. In one month a youngster may explore more footpaths than a veteran can traverse in one year. Nor is age the only differencer of persons. Some householders live like eremites, unconcerned with their fellow-villagers, uncurious about the countryside, ignorant of local life and lore. Others share the communal activities, and walk the county footpaths.

Despite differences of age and temperament, however, certain general laws govern the business of getting to know a district. The new house, for instance, may reveal idiosyncrasies which the former occupant did not consider worth mentioning, viz., a damp patch under the kitchen sink, or a smoking chimney, or a draught from the attic. If, moreover, you discovered the house in June, but did not occupy it until March, your first impressions will need to be revised, especially when the lane is waterlogged, and a loose slate has shattered the bathroom window. After a few days you meet some other surprises, further afield. Fox Covert, you learn, offers a short cut to the post office; the thrice-weekly milkman is a grandmother; the soggy area behind the greenhouse is not a geological freak, but a legacy from an Edwardian cesspit. No less surprising, on Thursday afternoons the fish shop in the market square becomes a branch of Regional Savings Bank Ltd., while Maison Colette is French for "Mrs Huggins", the dustman's wife. Helped, perhaps, by the vicar, you begin to meet your neighbours, who, like an onion, consist of several façades. Gradually—during drinks before dinner, or while leaning on a stile—you uncover the recent thrombosis, the Dunkirk DSO, the divorce, the bankruptcy, the *ménage ` trois*. And still the surprises multiply. The owner of the idyllic thatched cottage is a drunkard who beats his children; the curate used to be a lieutenant-colonel; the bookish couple are ersatz bores; and old Miss Mac (whom you took for a tedious nonentity) was the first woman ever to climb Mont Rouge. Likewise, some of your own façades are removed, often in a manner which amazes the whole family, as, for example, when you find that the villagers know exactly how much you paid for the house and precisely how much you can afford to spend on the alterations. Was it, you wonder, a postman —or could it have been the part-time washer-up—who informed the district that your mother lives at Salisbury, that your sister is expecting her second child, and that you have an account with Harrods?

All in all, the process of settling down is rather like learning to ride a bicycle. There are trials-and-errors; days when the elusive expertise seems to lie forever out of reach; and then, almost without knowing it, you find that you are no longer wobbling, no longer falling, no longer colliding. You are cycling. Just so, after about a year, when a stranger asks the way to the cross-roads, you instinctively reply: "Oh, you mean Kate's Corner." When the in-laws arrive, you recount several facts that were imparted by a farmer who had been born in what is now your bedroom. "At one time," you explain, "the hall formed part of a dairy. And on the other side of the lane just beside the gate, there used to be a cottage belonging to a widow. Old Mother Mug-wump, they called her. She kept a sweet shop in the parlour. She's still alive by the way. In fact we met her last week, coming out of the almshouse. Extraordinary to think she can remember Queen Victoria's funeral. The what? Oh no, it hasn't been a vicarage since the canon died. Some rather nice people live there now. The husband is a judge. But, of course, they've only been in the district for nine years."

When you yourself have been in the district for three years, the garden betrays the last of its secrets, which include a corner where the northerly gales uproot anything larger than a primrose. By this time too you have decided that the Smiths are snobs and that the Bulkley-Gordons are your friends for life. Although you arrived less than a year before he retired, you still miss the butcher who used to make his own sausages; and by the end of the fourth year you begin to wonder how on earth you will manage when old Perks can no longer trim the hedges. It seems ages since you ceased to call him "Mr Perks", and adopted his customary name of "Perky". You smile wryly on receiving an invitation to the wedding of a girl who, when you first arrived in the district, was starting to learn algebra.

If you are on the sunny side of forty, your new home has at last lost some of its novelty. If you are on the shady side of sixty, you may still miss the old familiar faces. But you will be unfortunate indeed if the day does not dawn when—returning from a holiday—you reach the bend in the lane and then the gate to the house, and are suddenly warmed by the sight thereof, as though the dog had come out to greet you, wagging his tail. There is nothing remarkable in this upsurge of affection. Birds experience it, or something akin to it, when they reach their nest. Dogs experience it when they see their basket. Badgers experience it when they smell their sett. Most creatures feel most at ease when most at home. Some people, on the other hand, seem almost impervious to the spirit of a place and the associations of an era. Uprooted every few years by economic necessity, they lack a firm hold anywhere. Not for them the love of home as Robert Bridges knew it:

> And through all change the smiles of hope amend
> The weariest face, the same love changed in nought ...

For many householders the acquisition of a home is either an alpha or an omega. With his arm around a waist, the young newcomer says: "This is where we shall start our life." With his arm around a shoulder, the elderly newcomer says: "This is where we shall end our days."

From Hell to High Heaven

One of my small fields is called Harepie, which I take to mean "a pie made of hares." In other words, the place was a poacher's paradise. Philology, however, may deceive the uninitiate. In theory, for example—though never in practice—a gazetteer of place-names might translate Harepie as: "Hare, from Old English *haer* or 'stony ground.' Pie is probably a variant of *Puy*, a local chief (cf. Weston Puy in the same county)." Nevertheless, I continue to believe that Harepie means what it appears to say, though why it should say so puzzles me because the field covers scarcely one-third of an acre, and is, in fact, no more than a triangular paddock. Was it formerly included in a much larger field where hares really did enjoy a living space? We shall never know, because we shall never discover when the property was divided by drystone walls.

Field-names often trace the extent to which husbandry has either advanced or remained static. Thus, the word "Devil" commonly connotes sour or infertile soil, as in Devil's Patch, Devil's Dingle, Devil's Furlong, Devil's Churchyard, Devil's Acre. Even when the land has been reclaimed, the old names abide, as in Devil's Own, Devil's Land, Devil's Bank, Devil's Tail. At the other extreme you will find a litany of grateful paeans, as in Mont Prosperous, Mount Pleasant, God's Garden, High Heaven, Paradise, Providence, Fillpockets, Bountiful, Promised Land, Canaan, Milk-and-Honey, Pound of Butter. Once again, however, a non-philologist may misinterpret the true meaning of a field-name and also of a regional name. Herefordshire's Golden Valley acquired its soubriquet when the Normans misread the name of the local river, writing Our as D'Or or "Gold." The valley therefore became "golden," and the river became D'Or and ultimately Dore. Likewise the Berkshire village of Britwell Salome has no connection with Herod's gruesome dancing girl. Britwell, the place with a bright stream, took its surname from Aumaricus de Suleham, who held the manor in 1236; and *his* family may have taken its name from Sulham, another Berkshire manor.

What are we to make of Egypt and Gibraltar in England's

green and pleasant land? Were the fields so-named by immigrants from those distant places? Were they named by Englishmen who have travelled thither? Probably not, for such fields usually lie on the perimeter of farms, and their names are synonyms for remoteness, as in Moscow, Mount Sinai, Nineveh, No Man's Land, Furthest, Beyond, Land's End, World's End, Utter End, Distant, Hem, Skirts. Sometimes the name dates the baptism, as in New York, North Carolina, Isle of Elba, Spioncop. Nineteenth-century farmers were fond of naming their fields after a famous battle: Trafalgar, Waterloo, Balaclava, Inkerman, Sebastopol. Near the Scottish border in Northumberland an undefined acreage is still named after the battle that took place there, Flodden Field. Some fields perpetuate what is best described as an intimate anonymity: Clancy's, Piper's, David's Furlong, Peg's Patch, Father's Acre.

Many fields recall a rural benefactor, as when the rent or produce of Holybread was bequeathed to provide part of the Sacrament. Lamplands likewise provided "a light to lighten the Gentiles" in church. Other specific benefactions were described by fields called Quire, Vestry, Chancel, Bellrope, L'Aisle, Vicar, Sexton, Priest, Glebe, Widows, Orphan. In the years when parish boundaries were imprinted on young minds via young backsides ("beating the bounds"), certain fields marked a halting place at which the parson either said a prayer or recited a passage from the Bible. The fields then acquired such names as Paternoster, Gospel, Amen Corner, Prayer Plot, Allelujah, Boundary Piece, Praise God, Parish Pride. Other fields utter an ominous echo, like the one near East Stoke in Nottinghamshire, which is still called Dead Man's Field because it marks the site where Lambert Simnel and his rebels were defeated by the King's army.

Field-names pose many questions, not all of which are linguistic. Did Greedy Guts consume vast amounts of fertiliser, or did it yield large quantities of crops? Did Cuckold's Haven receive its extra-marital name because of one man's disillusion, or because it was a communal Lovers Lane? Which of two bad neighbours owned Quarrelsome? How much clay went to the naming of Treacle? Who were the weary tillers of Labour-in-Vain, Mount Misery, Mount Famine, Cheat All, Starve Mouse, Hunger Hill, Cold Comfort, Old Misery, Break Back, Empty Furrow? Who were the happy husbandmen of Beans-and-Bacon, Long Gains,

D

New Delight, All's Well, Largesse, Lucky, Plenty Patch, Feast-field, Ripeness, Riches?

Our forefathers had a flair for attaching poetical names to prosaic facts. Muddy Corner vividly describes the crossroads where three field-gates allow cattle to churn a wintry surface. Marl, too, describes itself concisely; as also do the squelching Squob, Slob, and Quob. Equally concise, though now confused by changes in the language, is Brickfield, the *brec* or plot of land that had been broken-up for cultivation. Five Days Math is a meadow whose *math* or mowing lasted from Monday till Friday. Twelve Days Work is a field that could be ploughed in a dozen days. Pastures near a road were apt to announce their charges to drovers seeking overnight enclosure for livestock: Halfpenny Piece, Threepenny Patch, Tenpenny Close. The same practical poetry defined the shape of a field: Brandy Bottle, Cocked Hat, Leg of Mutton, Halfmoon, Sugar Loaf. Small fields received appropriate names, such as Thimble, Mousehole, Handkerchief Piece, Little Bit, Tiny, Pinpoint, Child's Yard. At other times such fields suffered a classical and facetious overstatement: Hundred Acres, Thousand Furlongs, Million Roods.

By uprooting their hedges and by demolishing their walls, some farmers have provided material for a new generation of field-namers. A topographer in the year 2077 may find himself descanting on the aptness of Windworn, Hedgeless, Six Months Math, and Ten Mile Meadow.

4

April Anthems

If it is true that the best things in life are free, then it is true also
that some of those boons must be sought, and sought quickly,
before they vanish. Among them is the zenith of birdsong, which
can be heard only at sunrise during April and May, the season of
mating and domesticity, when the birds resemble a choir, some
of whose members are more gifted than others. In choosing
Villon as the supreme lyric poet—"the head of all our choir"—
Swinburne found himself contradicted by those who preferred
Herrick or Heine. A similar subjectivity must condition our
opinion of birdsong, though few will deny that blackbirds sing
beautifully. Tennyson gladly sacrificed a corner of his garden in
exchange for the sound of their song:

> Oh, blackbird, sing me something well;
> While all the neighbours shoot thee round,
> I keep smooth plots of fruitful ground,
> Where thou may'st warble, eat, and dwell.

Nightingales, too, enjoy a high reputation, partly because their
Nachtmusik is heightened by the general silence. Even so, many
people find the song melancholy. Hearing it, Keats fell "half in
love with easeful Death." As a rule, it is the small birds that sing
most sweetly. Wordsworth's "little English robin" is a favourite
among countryfolk, for whereas some other birds cannot endure
our winter, the redbreast is an all-the-year-rounder, willing to
sing for his supper on Christmas Eve. Robert Bridges admired a

linnet "courting his lady in the spring." Walter de la Mare praised the wren alike for his nest and his song:

> Never was sweeter seraph hid
> Within so small a house . . .

Fondness for a specific breed may arise from old acquaintance, as among people living near an estuary, who tend to admire Masefield's widgeon flying over the marshes.

> Wing-linked. Necks a-strain,
> A rush and a wild crying.

Likewise there are sportsmen who regard the grouse's gruff call as the voice of a bird of paradise, while others respond to the curlew, that embodied spirit of mountains and moors. A sailor, on the other hand, may feel that no song excels the mew of gulls wheeling and dipping above blue water. Theirs is the last land-voice he hears when casting-off, and the first when dropping anchor. A gull's cry is the sea's *obbligato*, the very timbre of brine and beach and boats. To the young it reveals new horizons; to the old it utters ancient landfalls. Sometimes a preference embraces several species according to circumstance. Roaming the hills on an April morning, one may choose a skylark as nonpareil. Meredith compared the song with a series of ripples,

> All intervolved and spreading wide
> Like water-dimples down a tide . . .

Roaming the valleys on a November day, one may give the sparrow his due. Skelton compared the song with a *Nunc Dimittis*:

> He shall be the priest,
> The requiem mass to sing . . .

If two notes really do compose a song, then cuckoos may claim to be the voice of spring, despite their parasitic parenthood and a tendency to croak when June arrives. Beethoven echoed the cuckoo in his Pastoral Symphony, and Delius honoured it with a serenade. Gilbert White's musical friend discovered that cuckoos sing in different keys: "about Selborne Wood," White wrote, "he found they were mostly in D: he heard two sing together, the one in D, the other in D sharp . . . and about Wolmer-forest some in C." But birdsong is not the only voice of spring, for lambs can sound more insistent than cuckoos. Bleating and frisking, they were Wordsworth's delight, fit to rank with warblers and thrushes:

> Then sing, ye Birds, sing, sing a joyous song!
> And let the young lambs bound
> As to the tabor's sound!

Although the wind lowers its voice in April, the *pianissimo* is taken-up by leaves which create Cowper's "whispering sound of the cool colonnade." Tractors improvise modernly on an old theme, especially when February's fill-dyke has deluged a March sowing. In April, too, the droning bee seeks nectar while the sun shines. Quietest of all, a butterfly beats the air with tympanic wings, fluttering above streams that sing to a shower. Leverets, badgers, fox cubs, foals . . . each in its fashion harmonises with the silence of rising sap and the shrillness of homing rooks. In more domestic tones the lawn mowers whirr, the hoes clink, and the children forsake the class room in order to undertake a literal field study, adding their own blitheness to the birds'. Robert Browning summed it up:

> Oh, to be in England
> Now that April's here.

Those nine words speaks for the average man in average mood; the man you meet in the lane; the reticent man, not given to excessive originality; the man who means what he says: "Treat to be alive on a day like this." Elsewhere, of course, there are those for whom "April is the cruellest month." Immersed in private distress, they wince at the gaiety around them; laughter becomes a kind of blasphemy, and cheerfulness seems selfishness. As Joseph Conrad discovered: "There are circumstances when the sunlight may grow odious." Yet some wounds do heal, and many sorrows make their peace with Time. Therefore a country-man in April is out and about, marvelling as much at the music as at the mystery which shrouds the whole Creation.

A Tribute to the Ladies

Like hardy perennials, they withstand all weathers. Unlike perennials, they may blossom at any time of year, so that an August flower show sees them in full bloom, and a January jumble sale is warmed by their many-coloured headscarves. Cynics mock them, sentimentalists idealise them, but Nature confirms their role as the matrix or basic moulder of mankind. I refer, of course, to the farmwives and cottage mothers who in their youth raised six children on a weekly income that was less than their grandson's pocket money.

See them as they pick-and-choose among the stalls on market day, shaking grey heads in bewilderment when they pay more for one meal than they used to pay for a week's housekeeping. Though some of them are wizened and some infirm, many are still active, blessed with a roses-and-cream complexion envied by their teenage great-niece, a legacy of walking three miles to the shops and then three miles home again, lugging two heavy baskets while shepherding a footsore child. On special occasions their finery is a lesson in the art of growing old gracefully. The frocks are often homemade and therefore less uniform than mass-produced garments; the shoes are made to last rather than to pinch; and the hats sometimes bear a cluster of wax fruit. Hearing their conversation, a townsman might misread their character: "Fifty pence? Why, at South Molton I can buy the same thing for thirty-eight, and they'm a sight fresher than the stuff you'm selling" … "I've no patience with Evan Prys's daughter. She lies in bed till dinnertime and then comes home for an early breakfast" … "A body canna' hae his cake unless he bakes it. That's what I told him. My ain man offered ye a job, I said, but ye wouldna' take it. Try doing a day's work for a change, and then maybe ye'll no' need to come begging for your bairns." But when genuine distress does call, the no-nonsense girls give it, pressed down and overflowing. Has there been an accident outside the chapel? Blankets and hot tea arrive in no time; and the odds are, one of the girls learned first aid fifty years ago. Has the elderly widow suffered a stroke? Depend upon it, she will not suffer alone. Somebody looks-in twice a day for a chat; somebody tidies up once a week; somebody's husband mows the lawn or chops the firewood. Has Evan Prys's daughter abandoned her illegitimate child? Depend upon it, Grannie is there, comforting the waif, tracing the father, informing the council.

Many a countryman—and many a townsman, too—remembers the devotion of his own mother who, by stretching herself almost beyond the limit, did make both ends meet, so that beef-dripping spiced the dry bread, and old clothes clad the new baby. In a less extreme form much of that unselfishness is now practised by the professional classes who stint themselves in order to assert their right to give the children a good education. Marriage, however, is not Eve's sole vocation. How many spinsters have dedicated themselves to caring for a relative, or tending the world at large, or serving a good employer faithfully?

In deep country the older women still bake the sort of bread that cannot be bought at a bakery; still make the sort of butter that never yet came from a factory. They still usher infants into the world, and veterans out of it. They cure the ham, and whiten the doorstep, and keep the parlour spicker than span. While liberated young mothers toil eight hours a day in a factory or in an office (and then wonder why their children end up as delinquents), the enslaved matrons take pride in making their home sweet and snug and succulent. Though they may never have heard of Freud, they know that the proper rearing of children is a full time occupation, not an off-duty hobby.

From Cornwall to Caithness those *femmes sages* speak with one voice: "Things were hard in the old days. More than once I've gone to bed hungry so's the little ones should have enough to eat. And my eldest died of a disease the doctors got rid of twenty years ago. But I still don't envy the young. Too many of 'em are always whining for more and never satisfied when they've got it. No, I don't regret being born eighty years ago. At least we never had bombs, and car accidents, and shooting in the streets, and schoolchildren yelling at their teacher, and one striker putting a whole factory out of work."

In the business of comparing past with present, persons of riper years have both an advantage and a disadvantage. On the one hand, they possess the experience which can reach an informed verdict; on the other hand, they suffer the occupational hazard of rose-tinting their own heydays. Nevertheless, a reasonably unbiased observer will agree that many young women nowadays would not and probably could not achieve the self-sacrifice and good housekeeping which enabled a third son or a fourth daughter to rise from their penurious cottage to a place in the government or a professorship in the university.

Peering through the window of a cottage, you will perhaps see an old woman staring into the fire; and your compassion may seem misplaced because, instead of mourning perished summers, the widow may be enjoying an aftermath of harvest-home:

> Such the women, past all praise,
> Who with skin and bone defied
> Anxious nights and toilsome days;
> Britain's mother, Britain's bride.

Saddle Soap and Curry Combs

The saddler's shop overlooks the main street of a small town in the west country. Its windows display saddle soap and curry combs, wallets and stirrups, halters and satchels, purses and belts,

some of which are made on the premises. The walls above the
saddler's workbench are enlivened by prints of famous huntsmen
and notable stallions. In the background stand a pile of hides,
and sundry tackle awaiting repair. Brown leather is used for
saddlery, but the harness for a draught horse is made of leather
that has been dyed black on the grain or outer side, so that it

can be greased and thereby preserved without harming the colour.

The saddler's bench is littered with the tools of his trade, which include a half-moon knife for cutting the seat, flaps, and skirt of a saddle; a plough-gauge for slicing girth straps; a wooden mallet for shaping horse-collars; a creaser for marking marginal indentations; an edger for bevelling leather; and a stitch-wheel for piercing stitch-holes. In short, a saddler's shop is to horsemen as a chandler's shop to seamen. Simply by entering, a customer feels as though he had set one foot in the stirrups; and if he happens to be an old farmhand he will box the compass of a horse's collar . . . tug-chain, martingale, crupper strap, headstall.

The saddler himself is an elderly man, tending now to plumpness. His round and ruddy features are wrinkled about the eyes, but nowhere furrowed. His face, in fact, resembles a kind of human sun, radiating cheerful warmth. You might liken him to a Mr Pickwick, whose eyes are still so keen that they need no spectacles, not even for stitching a bridle. Life has dealt gently with him, partly because he has dealt gently with life. His wife, his children, and his grandchildren vie with his work as a source of unfailing happiness; and not even Bertrand Russell could have destroyed his faith in God.

Like every true craftsman, the saddler is proud of his skill, though for modesty's sake he uses the royal "We" when praising his own achievements. The other day, for instance, he showed me a pair of bellows that he had patched. "Us'm real pleased with this 'en," he confessed. "Been dropped in the fire, see? And th' owner were terrible upset. Her told me 'twas a hairloom from King George II. 'Well,' I said, 'it may have been a hairloom once, but in its present state I don't reckon as anyone would give 'ee above a tanner for 'en.' Still . . ." he fingered the well-stitched wounds . . . "us got to work, and now 'tis good enough for Old Nick to puff around with."

More fortunate than some of his kind, the saddler lives in a region where horses have not been wholly outpaced by petrol. Many farmers keep their own hunter; several employ Suffolks or Clevelands; shepherds go the rounds astride an Exmoor pony; and the staghounds and foxhounds ensure that leather and steel are still in demand, even although the average customer can no longer afford the luxury of craftsmanship. "No one," says our saddler, "could compete with the factories. It'd take me hours to do a job that these yere machines rattle through in five minutes. But mass-production never will make a masterpiece. Of course, if you say that aloud you'll have all the factories in England on your tail. But 'tis true. Why else does her ladyship stipulate hand-sewn and tip-top?" Then he points to a saddle hanging from the wall. "Forty year ago I made that saddle, and there's life in 'en yet. But nowadays 'tis near impossible to get hold of a really good hide. Some o' the stuff they call leather I wouldn't use as sticking plaster. And as for the price . . . well, if the trade unions keep on trying to keep pace with the cost o' living they'll soon be the only people who can afford to live."

Writing of rural craftsmen in Victorian England, George Bourne remarked: "they went about their work placidly, un-hurriedly, taking time to make their products comely." Our own saddler maintains that tradition. If you bespeak a belt, or a bridle, or a pair of leggings, he will say: "Come back in a month, and we'll see if 'tis ready." Yet there is nothing idle nor haphazard in his methods. One glance at the pile of repairable objects enables him to set an approximate delivery date. His book-keeping is rather notebook-keeping than double entry filing. Having written the customer's name on a small piece of cardboard, he ties it to the bellows, or the handbag, or the halter.

Sometimes an old crony stands beside him as he works, reviving their heydays. "I was colonel's galloper at the time," a greybeard remembers, "and I said to the corporal o' horse, 'Kaiser or no Kaiser, I'm not retreating another inch till I've drawn my full rations and a new nosebag.'" On market days the saddler's shop attracts people from outlying farms; women as well as men. Some seek a dog comb; others, a pair of stirrups; others, a patch for their hold-all. Then indeed the country talk confirms the present while recalling the past. "Can 'ee mend the strap on my tran-sistor?" . . . "Granfer gave me this belt. The buckle's come adrift" . . . "What's the price o' leather bootlaces nowadays?" . . . "Jute's all right, boy, but when it comes to leading a bull I put my trust in rope, same as Jacob did when he climbed his celestial ladder."

Fine weather or foul, the saddler keeps his working hours, lit in winter by an electric bulb, and shaded in summer by a striped awning above the window. Like Frank Kendon's carpenter, he remains unmechanised:

His hands are engines, and his eye
His gauge to measure beauty by . . .

The tang of a hide, the thump of a mallet, the clink of a spur, the pride of a craftsman; all are on show at the saddler's shop, warmed by the cheerful countenance of a man who radiates wisdom, simplicity, and benevolence.

Dialect and Dialogue

The tones of English country talk are unique. No other nation offers such a wide variety within such a narrow compass. Simply by crossing the River Tees at Piercebridge a stranger will detect a difference between the accent on the Durham bank and the accent on the Yorkshire bank. And if he proceeds north-east into Tyneside he will overhear words which to him might be double-Dutch or treble-Welsh. Whence came this melic Babel, this Pentecost of regional tongues? It came from our hybrid ancestry —the Celts, Jutes, Angles, Saxons, Vikings, Normans—whose speech during the Middle Ages was represented by five major dialects, each being either wholly or partly incomprehensible to speakers of the others. Dialects, in fact, were separate languages, not merely local words and accents. In its extreme form this separateness continued until the seventeenth century, when, for the benefit of parishioners who spoke no English, several Cornish parsons still held services in the old Cornish language.

Although philologists long ago traced the history of English dialects, one may doubt that anybody ever will discover why the accents vary so widely and with such curious narrowness. Fifty years ago the voice of an old North Buckinghamshire farmhand sounded almost unintelligible to people from other counties. Even more remarkable, accents may differ within a single county. More remarkable still, whence came the Northumbrian speech defect which Defoe described as "a difficulty in pronouncing the letter *r*"? More remarkable even than that, why is the difficulty confined to certain areas of Northumberland?

Interest in regional speech is relatively modern. Horace, for example, never tried to reproduce the patois of his Sabine shepherds, nor did Aeschylus descend from a wellbred sublimity.

Aristophanes sometimes indulged slang, but he never went beyond a version of "Get lost", which in his day was "Chuck yourself to the crows." One feels, too, that Racine and Pope were congenitally incapable of rusticating their Alexandrines. This preoccupation with the upper classes was partly justified because the lower classes, being illiterate and as a rule without much influence, were inherently undramatic. Shakespeare knew better, though he never swung to the other extreme by pretending that Bardolph and Pistol were more "significant" than Hamlet and Coriolanus. He may indeed have gone backstage to rehearse his own Warwickshire accent with Dogberry and Verges, but he did not write their parts phonetically. He relied rather on characterisation than on intonation, as, for instance, when a stolid country gentleman (the aptly named Shallow), delivers a profound platitude and then he ends with a reference to fat stock prices: "Certain, 'tis certain; very sure, very sure; death, as the Psalmist saith, is common to all: all shall die. How a good yoke of bullocks at Stamford fair?"

It was the industrial revolution which set a self-conscious wedge between town and country, and ultimately led some writers to suppose that the ordinary people are more remarkable than the extraordinary, so that highborn heroic characters were replaced by nonentities in a bed-sitter. When evil communications began to corrupt our regional speech, we sent professors to tape-record the dying echoes. Accents will survive awhile—perhaps for a long while—but most of the old words have perished.

Tennyson was a pioneer among recorders of country talk, as in *The Northern Farmer*:

> Wheer 'asta beän so long and mea leggin 'ere aloän?

William Barnes went further than that, sacrificing a talent for poetry to a flair for philology. His *Poems of Rural Life in the Dorset Dialect* contains more than three hundred pieces loaded with local words and quasi-phonetic spellings which cannot be understood without constant reference to a glossary. It was not his fault that "Zummerzet and zider" are now employed by the entertainment industry to represent the voice of rural England southward from Oxfordshire:

> While zome, a-gwain from pleäce to pleäce,
> Do daily meet wi' zome new feäce . . .

Barnes's friend and admirer, Thomas Hardy, preferred a less literal version of local speech, as when a yokel tells the mayor of Casterbridge: "I seed en go down street on the night of your worshipful's wedding . . ." Hardy stated his own ends and means in a letter to *The Athenaeum*: "An author may be said to fairly convey the spirit of intelligent peasant talk if he retains the idiom, compass, and characteristic expressions, although he may not encumber the pages with obsolete pronunciations . . ." Hardy did not approve Barnes's phonetic texts: "If," he said, "a writer attempts to exhibit on paper the precise accents of a rustic speaker, he disturbs the proper balance of a true representation . . ." Some representations can be achieved solely by means of word-inversion. Thus, whereas an English farmer will say: "I shouldn't be surprised if it rains tonight," a Welsh farmer will say: "There'll be rain tonight, I shouldn't wonder." In Scotland the problem is difficult because, although many Scots say "bairthday" instead of "birthday," the word does not sound the same in Glasgow as in Skye.

Few readers will deny that an excessive use of phonetic dialogue becomes tedious and ultimately self-defeating. Most will agree that an occasional echo of rustic speech is allowable—is, indeed, necessary—to any prolonged utterance by a rustic speaker. In the last resort, readers must rely partly on their aural imagination and partly on the writer's mastery of art, which alone can tell him how to use the vernacular.

Boys of the New Brigade

While the siren was still wailing, the butcher whipped off his blue and white apron, and ran across the street, hotly pursued by the baker's assistant, who was wiping the dough from his hands. Fifteen seconds later a sports car skidded into the square, and out jumped the garage mechanic. Then, like a deflated bagpipes, the siren subsided, though not the excitement. Women leaned from open windows. Shoppers clustered in doorways. Small boys and barking dogs raced to the fire station while an off-duty constable stood at the cross roads, ready to clear the way.

Presently a second car arrived, followed by a cyclist speeding from the sawmill beyond the bridge. Since the fire chief worked opposite the fire station, the scarlet-framed doors were already open, and the engine ticking-over. Three more cars appeared, and the occupants were soon donning their uniforms.

"Where is it, bach?" the mechanic shouted.

"Pont-y-rhydd," replied the chief. "Dai's place. Two hayricks blazing, and the house threatened." He turned to the latest arrival. "Come on, Morgan, man. You can button-up on the way. Idris arrived yet? Good. It's seven miles, remember, and three gates to open when we start climbing near Maes Mawr."

Less than six minutes have elapsed since Dai Davies dialled 999, yet the fire engine has already crossed the bridge, and is hooting its way through a flurry of April sleet. In the market square, meanwhile, business returns to normal. Women shut their windows. Shoppers collect their wares. And a small boy with a stop watch cries: "You've lost your bet, Dewi. They were only three seconds outside the record. They'd have beaten it if the Jones's cat hadn't got in the way."

Rounding a bend at Cwm Clotty, the fire engine—or, rather, the retired shepherd—has a narrow escape. "If they'd told me they were coming," he complained, "I'd have switched-on my deaf aid." At Newydd Plas a hen is killed, and at the second gate a fireman is grazed, but the driver knows every inch of the slippery route.

"Not far now, lads," shouts the chief. "I can see the smoke. Let's hope he's got his grannie to safety. She'll be ninety on Thursday. Give 'em another toot, Morgan. Let 'em know we're coming." He glances at the youngest volunteer. "Cliff, my son, remember what I said last time . . . don't brandish your axe like you were a Red Indian. Just concentrate on the water aspect."

But there are no Dogberry nor Verges on board the fire engine. Calmly and quickly a hose is dragged to the pond. Soon the pumps drone, the water gushes, the flames dwindle. "Idris!" calls the chief, "get a ladder on the roof. I can see something smouldering. And you, Rhys, nip round the shippon. He keeps his paraffin there. Who? Says what? Lord save us, tell grannie I'll sign her autograph book when we've finished."

Half-an-hour later the blackfaced firemen sip tea in the kitchen while their chief holds a post mortem. "You ought to have known better, Dai. Anyway, I thought you'd given it up. It was a narrow escape you've had. If this wind had freshened, the whole roof might have gone." He walks toward the old woman. "Well, gran, my love, who says nothing ever happens on the mountain? All the same, I hope you'll tell that grandson of yours not to chuck his fag ends in the straw. Twice in two years he's nearly given himself an illuminated address. And now where's that autograph book?" He unscrews a fountain pen. "There you are. Name, initials, and B.A., Lampeter." He returns the gold-lettered volume. "You'll notice I've added a postscript with special reference to Pont-y-rhydd ... 'There's never a fire without fag ends.' "

On the way home they notice that the dead hen has disappeared. "That'll be Evan Jenkins," someone says. "He'll retrieve a pheasant before you've shot it. Anything to avoid a day's work, that Evan's motto. It was the same with his father and his grandfather. The nearest they ever came to soiling their hands was in the workhouse, and even there they decided to develop rheumatism."

This time the old shepherd sees the brigade approaching. "Dai again, I shouldn't wonder," he mutters. "Whenever the market's bad he goes up in flames."

Back at the station, the chief has a reminiscent word with young Cliff Gwilym. "If that had happened when Dai's gran was a girl, the whole house would have caught fire. They'd no telephone up there in those days, and the nearest engine ... well, there wasn't one." He pauses. "Hey, what's wrong with your thumb?"

"Thumb?" says Cliff. "Oh, just a slight burn."

"Burn be damned. It's bleeding. Were you waving that blasted axe?"

"It was the rough end of the ladder, that's all. We must have broken the record, surely? Not like the old days when they'd only a makeshift engine. My great-granda said he used to drive the horses for it."

"Then your great-granda lied. There was only one horse, and only when it wasn't ploughing. It made a brave show, though."

"You saw the horse?"

"Boy, I am bald, I know it. But do you suppose I have been a part-time fireman for ninety years? Still, they did their best. They'd a great brass boiler on board, see? And they lit a furnace under it, and if they were lucky the steam pump was working when they reached the blaze. And if they were very lucky indeed, they found some water within half-a-mile of the house. But I'm telling you, Cliff Gwilym, not even in their most fortunate moments did they try to scalp the survivors."

5

All in the Month of May

In order to pass as a naturalist one must offer something better than the ability to recognise a bullfinch and to know that its bones are more or less hollow. If you wish to test your knowledge of such matters, spend half-an-hour with a man who has spent half a century dissecting zebras, fieldmice, crocodiles, pythons, and parrots. Nevertheless, a layman is free to make his own observations, even although a correct interpretation of them belongs to the expert. For example, do some birds sing more sweetly than others of the same species? Beyond doubt they seem to do so. No less certainly, their apparent prowess may be an illusion, caused by circumstances that are irrelevant to the song itself. I can recall two such illusions. The first occurred at a point where the road from Great Missenden to Chequers Court indulges a double bend near the foot of Cobblers Hill in Buckinghamshire. I was walking at the time, burdened by private affairs, and blinkered by a February mist which made the winter appear eternal. Suddenly—so loud and so close that the sound startled me—suddenly an invisible blackbird sang his first song of the year. Neither then nor thereafter did I rate the song as unusually sweet, yet I still regard it as the most beautiful I ever heard in winter.

The second illusion occurred during May, at a point where the Roman road near Craven Arms passes under a bridge *en route* for Leintwardine in Herefordshire. Again I was walking in mournful weather, April having proved even wetter and wilder than a vile-tempered March. Moreover, I had lately arrived from

a fortnight's sojourn among the Scottish mountains, where
birds are less numerous than in England, less eager to proclaim
the spring. And then came a hailstorm. However, fate had granted
me a waterproof bridge, so I unslung the haversack, and consoled
myself with coffee and sandwiches. Afterwards, while lighting a
pipe, I became conscious of a brightness which could not possibly
have been caused by the matchstick. Glancing up, past the bridge's
dripping gloom, I saw that the clouds had passed, and for the
first time in many days the sun shone from a blue sky. At that
moment I heard the first cuckoo in spring, which still deceives
me into rating it the sweetest I ever did hear.

Those unscientific attitudes were redeemed by several attempts
to discount the subjective or emotional factors. I remember, for
example, the song of a blackbird near Beaminster in Dorset.
Once more the month was May, and once more the sun shone,
though this time at eight o'clock in the evening, when my mood
was better tuned to the moment, for spring had fulfilled its
promise, and I was in the relaxed state of mind which is a reward
of bodily exercise. Leaning on a gate, gazing westward at the
radiant greenscape, I heard a blackbird whose song so impressed
me that I wondered whether the circumstances had blunted my
critical faculty. But no amount of scepticism could avail. I thought
then, as I think now, that the song sounded richer and more
flutelike than any I had ever heard. If this really was so, then the
explanation lay with the bird's vocal equipment and with its
response to the events of the moment . . . a hearty meal, perhaps,
or an awareness that peace and plenty blessed the nest.

A comparable experience occurred while I was cruising offshore
from Saint Mawes in Cornwall. A shoal of bass lurked nearby,
and over the bass a cluster of whitebait, and over the whitebait
a whirlpool of gulls, one of which flew toward my boat and then
circled above it, as though in salutation, all the while piping like
a bo'sun. To some people, no doubt, the gulls' mewing seems
melancholy; few would describe it as a song; and none would
rank it with the voice of a nightingale. Yet on that sunny May
morning the cry of that gull sounded more melodious than any
that had ever greeted my landfalls.

Similar impressions can be received via the senses of sight and
scent, for it was in May that I met the most profuse and fragrant
hawthorn blossom while climbing Offa's Dyke at a point near

Middle Knuck Farm, a thousand feet among the Shropshire larks. Some of the hawthorn trees were fifteen feet high, standing in isolation; others were set close enough to form a white-topped hedge; and whenever a breeze stirred them, the petals drifted down like scented snowflakes. On that occasion I walked with two fellow-travellers, each of whom agreed that they had never before seen such rife blossom on such green hills under such blue skies.

It would indeed be interesting to discover all the reasons why Caruso and the Beaminster blackbird excelled their peers. Possessed of such knowledge, we might use it in order to improve our own talents. Science meanwhile is correct in observing the rules that are a condition of its proper functioning. Birdsongs are best analysed in a laboratory. The month of May, however, is not a laboratory. It is an open air invitation to adopt all manner of unscientific attitudes, including nostalgia, cheerfulness, awe, worship, love. There is a sense in which it does not greatly matter whether the phenomena are a cause, or an effect, of our delight. As Walter de la Mare remarked: "All writing *about* poetry cannot but resemble a beating of the air." Dissection plays only a minor role when springtime breeds the days which Robert Bridges set to music:

> Days, that the thought of grief refuse,
> Days that are one with human art,
> Worthy of the Virgilian muse,
> Fit for the gaiety of Mozart.

Over the Sticks

Many of the spectators knew one another because this was a parish point-to-point, attracting few strangers and none at all of the criminals who haunt professional race meetings. Laid across three fields by kind permission of Hillcrest Farm, the course was marked with whitewashed oil drums. The fences were a row of besom brooms, the water jump was a brook, two feet deep and four feet wide. Roped-off for weighing and saddling, a paddock adjoined the green marquee which served a triple role as beer tent, first aid post, and secretary's office. Two brown tents, marked respectively *Ladies* and *Gents*, stood on the perimeter, at a discreet distance from each other. Hidden under a huge peaked cap and a voluminous leather satchel, the car park attendant—a small boy—looked rather like a bus conductor who had shrunk in the wash.

From time to time a loudspeaker announced the details of each race and the state of play in the secretary's tent, so that "Miss Felicity Smith on Bonnie Lass" was followed by "Any of that whisky left?" . . . to which the crowd responded with a cheer. After some moments the loudspeaker was heard to say "Why the Hell didn't you *tell* me it was switched on?" Again the crowd cheered, whereat the loudspeaker crackled and died.

Only two bookmakers attended, each standing beside a blackboard on which the names and odds were continually chalked, erased, and re-chalked, rather as though a schoolmaster were having difficulty in solving his own equation. Both of the blackboards carried a printed sign, *Turf Accountant*, which led one child to suppose that the chalkers combined book-keeping with lawn mowing. In all other respects, however, this was a truly amateur occasion ("amateur" comes from a Latin word, denoting that the competitors rode for love, not for money). Party politics and national prestige were conspicuously absent. Likewise there were no fits of pique, no boasts of prowess, no disputes with stewards. This sporting camaraderie was strengthened by the weather, for whereas last year's events had been swept with heavy rain, this year the sun shone, as it did on Masefield's point-to-point:

> A wind blew by and the sun shone bright,
> Showing the guard rails painted white.
> Little red flags, that gusts blew tense,
> Streamed in the wind at each black fence.

And whenever the starter's flag came down, you heard

> A tide of horses in fury flowing,
> Beauty of speed in glory going . . .

Although horse racing is an ancient pastime, the word "steeplechase" did not appear until 1793, when it emphasised the fact that in those years a mounted obstacle race was aligned on a church, following a course whose natural hazards must be overcome, whether streams, walls, hedges, ditches, or gates. During the eighteenth century it became fashionable to wear a three-cornered hat when riding. What we call a jockey cap was worn only by servants and professional riders. The cap's ribbon—now merely ornamental—served to tie a postillion's *queue* or pigtail. King George III took to wearing a cap while on horseback, but in Squire Osbaldeston's time a number of masters of foxhounds still preferred soft hats. Many riders, therefore, must have ended their career by breaking their skulls. Ladies, of course, rode side-saddle, a graceful accomplishment which flourished until fashion decreed that women should become imitation men.

At a parish point-to-point the competitors dress informally. Some of them wear Newmarket boots and a tennis shirt; others choose leggings and a polo-neck sweater. During wet weather the farmers have been known to win despite their gumboots and oilskin. The sociological aspects are as varied as the sartorial, because the meeting reveals a cross-section of rural society. The announcer, for example, is a retired major from the Indian Army; the clerk of the course is a blacksmith; one of the stewards is a solicitor; and the timekeepers are respectively a publican and a dentist. Last year's winner of the Ladies Cup was a farmhand's daughter; this year's favourite is a baronet's sister. Arriving in a 1968 Morris, the squire glances enviously at the grocer's up-to-date Rover.

Whether it is held by the Brigade of Guards or by the Lunesdale Farmers, every amateur point-to-point sees the riders taking their fences as Lord Scamperdale took his own, "as if he had a spare neck in his pocket." Styles of riding vary. Younger competitors tend to crouch very low, as though avoiding a hail of bullets; but one of the veterans—who learned his horsemanship at Weedon—favours the old cavalry style and a rhythmic rocking-horse motion. Now and again a dark horse confounds the punters, as when the wild-eyed bay, having twice refused the first fence, takes the bit between his teeth, sails over every obstacle, and transforms a disastrous start into a three lengths victory.

When the last race has ended, the voice of experience is heard, explaining the difference between a fool's folly and a wise man's flutter. "Happen owd Jim Thwaite mun be feeling sore. We begged him to put his shirt on't, but all he said was, 'I did that last year, and I've been shivering ever since.' But we were reet an' all. Missus and me got the five bob back plus a quid for our trouble. And so did everyone else, except owd Jim. Still, I tried to cheer up the bookie. 'Tis nobbut a mug's game, I told him."

The Lark Ascending

Never before had I heard such a clamorous conclave of skylarks. They were singing when I arrived, singing when I lingered, singing when I left. How many sang I cannot say, because the sunlight dazzled all attempts to count them. But they were there, visible and audible, like a flock of pilgrims calling on heaven to open its azure gates; and below them lay the Selkirkshire hills, green as a gigantic golf course speckled with sheep.

The hour was noon, the zenith of a day so calm that the single white cloud resembled a ship at anchor on a blue lagoon. The turf was warm to touch, like an electric blanket. The sun had dispersed the early morning mist, but without creating a heat haze, so that you could see for miles, and the only things you saw were hills and sheep and one thorn tree lonely as a signpost beside a drystone wall flanking a drover's track. Somewhere behind those hills stood Walter Scott's Abbotsford, towered and turreted; but from my resting place no house was visible, nor indeed did any exist within an hour's walk. Meanwhile, the larks sang as if for my own benefit. Once or twice a bird went to earth, as in Quiller-Couch's pastoral England:

> O tired lark descending on the wheat!

But whereas Q. reached Eckington Bridge at sunset, these noon-day larks descended solely in order to prepare for another nine hours of song. Sometimes a bird sprang up, as though from a catapult, singing while it soared; but one bird rose silently, and, having reached the topmost rung of its flight, hovered there, still speechless. Then, with a steep curtsy, it let loose the lyric which poets can render only as black marks on a white page:

> He sings the sap, the quickened veins,
> The wedding song of sun and rains ...

This was not a brief outburst, a mere interlude between prolonged silences. It had begun at dawn, as a laud to the rising sun.

It would end at dusk, as a compline to the starry west. Nor was
it reserved for summer. On the contrary, you may hear a lark
singing at midnight in November. To some people the lark
sounds sweetest when it heralds the dawn; to others, when it
enlivens the noon; to others, when it serenades the sunset.
Morning, noon, or night ... spring is the season when the
paean sounds gayest, and deep country is the place where man-
made interruptions are least likely to mar the music. So, I basked

full-length on the warm grass of a remote hill, telling the time by using the thorn tree as a sundial; telling it reluctantly because shadows slant swiftly when moments are precious.

Although the choir at last moved away, one singer still hovered overhead. Fixing my attention on him, I timed his song, which lasted for more than three minutes, until the bird sheered away and fell like a stone to the ground. Could human lungs maintain such a rapt and vibrant tremolo? Could they excel the lark that was once heard to sing without a pause for eighteen minutes? Presently the bird perched himself on a tussock of grass, and there for several seconds he sang full-throated, and might have continued had not my dog barked while dreaming.

Even the sober textbooks break into a kind of poetry when they describe the skylark's song: "profuse, unpremeditated art, delivered soaring almost vertically to 1,000 feet." The same book adds that the birds are to be found on "open ground, preferably arable." For two hours the Selkirkshire songs went on, sometimes near, sometimes not so near, yet always with tireless intensity. Small wonder that the poets chose a skylark as their talisman of joy. To Chaucer the bird was "the messenger of day"; to Daffyd ap Gwilym, "a priest at High Mass"; to Shakespeare, the singer "at heaven's gate"; to Milton, the singer "in spight of sorrow"; to Shelley, "a blithe Spirit"; to Wordsworth, "the happiest bird"; to G. M. Hopkins, "cheer and charm"; to Margaret Howard, "the sun's emissary." If music is indeed poetry, then the song of a skylark justifies Mallarmé's claim: "Il n'y a que le Beauté—et elle n'a qu'une expression parfaite—la Poésie." Hearing the song, I likened it to the sound of the birds of Rhiannon, a music so mellifluous that "fourscore years passed as a day in listening to them, and there was no remembrance of sorrow whatsoever."

Far below, the drove road gleamed like a darker version of the surrounding pastures, empty and obsolete, though for centuries a highway on which livestock travelled south to Jedburgh and Carlisle and London. How resoundingly those hills had echoed to the barking dogs, the shouting horsemen, the thudding hooves, and the bleat and moo of their cargo. How recently the pageant had faded. Elderly countryfolk can remember the years when cattle and sheep were driven from Wiltshire to Norfolk via the Icknield Way through the Chilterns. Then came the ubiquitous lorry that carried the animals direct to market or to the nearest railway station. Now, therefore, the drove road was simply a short cut from one part of the Cheviots to another, or in summer a haven for fugitives from Matthew Arnold's "strange disease of modern life." Modern life, however, seemed irrelevant while the larks sang songs that had been perfected aeons ago; not, of course, to please the human ear, but to communicate with other birds in the business of mating and feeding and keeping alive. Yet those domestic messages do please the human ear, partly as evocations of summer, and partly as tidings of great joy, for it is difficult not to believe that the birds really are expressing conscious pleasure when they utter the music which Meredith set to words:

> Shrill, irreflective, unrestrained,
> Rapt, ringing on, the jet sustained
> Without a break, without a fall,
> Sweet-silvery, sheer lyrical . . .

Taking the Car for a Walk

When the weather smiles I sometimes take the car for a walk, by which I mean we amble at twenty-five miles an hour, frequently stopping to stare. The car itself has a hood which on warm days can be pulled back, enabling me to see the sun, to smell the hay, to hear the birds. So, while other motorists wilt inside their glass hearse, I feel the breeze on my face, and am content to average fifteen miles an hour, a leisurely speed that makes you the master, not the slave, of machinery. Duly submissive, your vehicle halts while you decide whether those foxgloves really are five feet tall. It moves slowly while you compare lowland Suffolks with hilltop Herdwicks. Patient as a donkey—and not much faster—it carries you to the summit whence you sight Tan Hill Inn, or Stane Street, or the roofs of Tomintoul. Instead of saving time, you spent it and also invest it as a hedge against the years' irremediable inflation.

On some journeys I follow familiar lanes, enjoying that sensation of ease which Edward Thomas relished when he wrote of "speeding in a car" along roads which one is accustomed to traverse slowly on foot. Since Thomas's speeding occurred in

1910, his pace was about the same as mine, but with this difference, that whereas he suffered the shouts of frightened pedestrians, I suffer the shouts of frightening motorists, for this generation assumes that speed confers comfort, and that comfort begets ease. But to drive fast is *not* necessarily to feel at ease. People who do drive fast are unobservant of anything except the traffic. The slower you drive, the stronger becomes your awareness of the effort of walking and the effortlessness of riding. Try driving at six miles an hour up a steep hill which you usually climb on foot at two miles an hour. Then indeed you will marvel at mechanical motion, far more so than if you were racing on a motorway.

My own kind of dawdling allows a countryman to keep abreast of the latest developments in his own district. He can, for example, study the farmers' timetable, noting who has already sown and who has not yet ploughed. He can discover where the riverside kingcups are in bloom and where the mountain ash has reddened its berries. In the course of one hour he shares a dozen brief encounters with neighbouring farmers and outlying cottagers. While meandering through unfamiliar lanes he follows his own radiator, lured on by signposts to Hell, High Heaven, Come-to-Good, Edith Weston, Mavis Enderby, Cherry Willingham, Martin Hussingtree, Saint Anthony-in-Roseland, Barton-on-the-Clay, Stanton-on-Hine-Heath, Hensington Within and Without, Langton-Juxta-Partney, Preston-upon-the-Weald-Moors, Pen Gloch y pibwr, Llangottock-vibon-Avel, Rose Ash, Drunken Bottom, Lud, Ide, Eye, Worf. If the signposts fail to sound lyrical, he can turn left because at the last crossroads he turned right, or because he has sighted a thatched cottage with honeysuckle under the eaves, or a man ploughing behind two horses, or a Saxon church, or a Norman castle, or a zigzag footpath to the sea.

If you dawdle through a strange countryside the surprises may prove mutual, as they did when I lately followed a lane (marked *Unfit For Motor Vehicles*) that heaved like a switchback, all the while growing grassier down the middle. In some places the top of the bank was three feet above my head; in other places the bank disappeared, revealing that a single false move might land me in the stream two hundred feet below. After about a mile I met a brown-bearded man who looked remarkably like Piers Plowman's younger brother. His headgear was not quite cap yet scarcely a trilby; his trousers were tied at the ankle with string; his jacket resembled a knee-length jerkin; and his ash stick was oozing sap.

"'T'aint yere," he warned me.

"What isn't?"

"The place you'm looking for."

"I'm not looking for a place."

The man received my simple statement as though it were an unanswerable question. Utterly bewildered, he scratched his neck, which caused the headgear to flop forward over his eyes. At last he said: "We don't often see anyone yereabouts. In fact, we haven't seen a stranger since ..." he paused, unable to remember.

"A week ago?" I suggested.

"'Twas more than a week. Must have been sometimes last September. A fella took this track 'cause someone had told 'en 'twas quicker. Said he'd come from Walsall, wherever that is. Had a smashing journey, he said. Averaged eighty-three on the motorway, and near forty down the lanes."

"He can't have averaged forty on this lane."

"He tried to. That's why the Hay-Hay sent a crane to haul 'en out o' the stream." The man pointed to a new gatepost beside the verge. "If that gate had been open he might have avoided the water but he wouldn't have recognised his headlights."

"And that was last year?"

"Somewhere around then. 'Twas harvest time ... that I do remember ... 'cause his rear wheel flattened my cider bottle."

At that moment a witchlike woman appeared, followed by three barefoot children, all of whom stared at me. "Who is he?" the woman asked. "Rates and taxes? Or just the cesspit?" While the husband shook his head the youngest child pointed at me, exclaiming: "Man! It's a man!"

No, they were not gipsies. They lived snugly and cleanly in a cottage beside the stream, cultivating a few acres of their own, and working part-time on a farm nearby.

Not every encounter is so bizarre as that one, but I have yet to take the car for a walk without meeting something humorous, or poignant, or historic, or beautiful.

6

Three Men Went to Mow

The Commander's farm includes one meadow which receives special attention, rather as though it were the sole piece of antique furniture in a modern house. While the other enclosures have each their own name—Belfry, Peg's Paddock, Two Furlongs, Farthing Piece—the special meadow is known simply as "the hayfield". Covering about three acres, it yields a heavy crop which can be scythed by two men in one day, but since the Commander himself lends a hand, the work usually ends in mid-afternoon.

Why is the meadow mown manually? "Because," the Commander will tell you, "I enjoy the exercise." That would seem a satisfactory answer if the Commander were a sedentary man, but since he spends much of his life working out of doors, another and deeper motive must be sought, for the truth is, he loves the skills of his youth, and regards the hayfield as an arena in which to wield a scythe. There is moreover a tradition about the hayfield. Villagers say that it was enclosed and irrigated three centuries ago, as an early example of a water-meadow. The first record of such irrigation occurred in 1610, when Rowland Vaughan published his *Most experienc'd and long-established Waterworks*, claiming that he had constructed several water-meadows along the Dore Valley in Herefordshire. During the 1850s a few sheep farmers were still making water-meadows on the Wessex chalklands. Then the sheep-folding era gave way to new methods which outdated artificial irrigation.

Mourning the hazards of his own profession, Elgar cried:

"God is against art". There are times when even a pious farmer suspects that God is against agriculture. Let the words of an honest eyewitness speak for themselves, like those of John Thorne, an Exmoor farmer, who in 1826 reported: "The Ground more burnt, hay scarcer." In 1827 he reported: "The most Grass this year ever known." And the year after that? A wet summer and the hay crop "disastrous." Half a century earlier, Gilbert White had reported that Hampshire farmers were trying to cut sodden hay in October. If, however, the sun does shine on well-watered soil, haytime can seem the sweetest season of the year, a blend of spring and summer, when the grasses are coming into flower, and the pollen dust is almost ready to fall, but the nourishment in the stem has not yet moved upward to help the ripening seed. "Gently does it" is the mower's motto because grasses are a fragile commodity, covered with a delicate film of waterproof wax which, if broken, will admit water into stems that already contain 75 per cent moisture. Green grass, in fact, becomes hay by losing moisture to sunlight and wind.

When at last the great day dawns, the Commander musters his crew, an ex-Marine and a retired naval rating, who, like himself, are nearer seventy than sixty years of age. With shirt sleeves rolled up, and his cap at a Beatty angle, the Commander runs a thumb across the gleaming scythe. Equidistant to port and starboard, the two hands wait a yard astern of their master. "Right!" One word suffices. The pageant begins.

There are many books about mowing, but only music can evoke the slow-motion sculpture of mowers and the rhythmic sibilance of scythes. Mowing is a type of rustic ballet, comparable with poplars swaying on a breeze. The act itself is so easy that centuries of simple men have mastered it, yet so difficult that an urban learner has been known to topple over at the first stroke and to gash his ankle at the second. Although outmoded, scythes are still a very private property among veteran farmworkers. Woe betide the child who removes the sacking from old Sam's blade. "How many times have I told 'ee? You'm not to meddle with 'en. I knew a little maid as lost both her legs just by looking at the handle." But Sam's kindly concern is in part a memory from his youth, when a man's scythe symbolised his livelihood, like a violinist's Stradivarius.

By mid-morning the Commander and his men are in mid-meadow, each leaving a swathe as straight as the wake of an unerring ship. They use the traditional English terms, saying that a load of old hay (which is dry) comprises thirty-six trusses weighing eighteen hundredweight, whereas a load of new hay (which is damp) weighs more than nineteen hundredweight. In most parts of England the hay is rated new until Michaelmas Day. In order to avoid rotting, the swathes are turned or tedded with a pitchfork; and this can be done next day if the sun is hot. Then the Suffolk Punch arrives with a mechanical rake which tosses the hay into wind-rows. During unsettled weather the rows are heaped and then turned next morning, but in ideal conditions the whole business ends on the third afternoon. Since the mowers' grandchildren are allowed to help with the carting, the final scene recalls John Clare's haytime:

> Boys loading on the waggon stand
> And men below with study hand
> Heave up the shocks with lathy prong
> While horse-boys lead the team along . . .

To build an efficient rick requires skill. Gabriel Oak, you remember, took especial care when protecting Bathsheba's hay against an impending storm; "He had stuck his ricking-rod, or poniard, as it was indifferently called—a long iron lance, polished by landling—into the stack, used to support the sheaves . . ." Lightning, however, is not the only threat to a hayrick, for the starch in the grass generates heat. If fermentation continues, the starch forms sugar, then alcohol, and finally acetic acid, liable to smoulder and catch fire. Fermentation ought therefore to be stopped at the sugar stage. The Commander never allows the temperature of his ricks to exceed 140 degrees Fahrenheit. When necessary, he cools them by cutting a hole through the hay. This obviates what the ex-Marine calls "infernal combustion."

Light and Shade

It is always pleasant when the sun shines, and never more so than after a dull spell in summer. The frequency and duration of those spells can be assessed only by consulting weather records over many years, for age tends to tint the spectacles of memory,

F

casting a rosy glow on childhood summers whose frost-bitten flowers were battered by rain. There is certainly no lack of evidence that Villon's *nèiges d'antan* sometimes overspill into May, and will occasionally sprinkle a few flakes on June. Charles Lamb, for example, offered wry comfort to all who huddle in windswept beach huts. "We have," he sighed, "been dull at Worthing one summer, duller at Brighton another, dullest at Eastbourne a third, and are now doing dreary penance at Hastings!" Even if the dullness sprang partly from a dislike of those resorts *qua* resorts, it still suggests that the weather itself was dull, because Lamb—a deskbound Londoner—loved the sun, and praised any place which basked in its temperate beams. Lamb's gloomy weather report may have evoked a protest from Chambers of Commerce, saying: "Had you been here last week . . ." or "The glorious weather during the month following your departure . . ." But our climate is so British that Lamb might have found the sun simply by strolling in search of it.

I remember a summer when I was living in *Noah's Ark*, a cable's length off Saint Anthony-in-Roseland, across the bay from Falmouth. It so happened that I had arranged (weather permitting) to take mid-morning coffee with friends at Portscatho, a few miles up-coast. Unfortunately, the day awoke in a black mood which turned so grey that I could scarcely see my own masthead. Tankers boomed mournfully in Carrick Roads, and the ferry crept past at four knots, slow as a lame ghost. While I was breakfasting, a landsman's launch grazed the clinker hull, causing me to spend the rest of the forenoon on watch, blowing a whistle whenever I heard the throb of an engine. At midday the mist lifted, but by that time my appointment was an hour overdue. Weather, in short, had *not* permitted.

Next day dawned idyllic, so I up-anchored, rounded the lighthouse, and was already halfway to Portscatho when I noticed what appeared to be smoke, drifting from the cliffs above Greeb Point. A second sighting showed that I was approaching a fog bank. Fortunately, I knew every yard of the coast. But I knew also that at low water the fairway into Portscatho might become a foulway, only a few yards wide and less than a fathom deep. Once inside, a mistbound boat would find it impossible to manoeuvre without either going aground or striking a rock. However, I was now more than halfway there, and in no mood to be defeated by thick weather. While visibility lasted I took a bearing, and thereafter trusted to memory. Then the mist closed-in, damp and grey and blind. Having steered seaward awhile, I spun the wheel, half-closed the throttle, and made for the shore. After about five minutes I stopped the engine. A car was audible, due west, climbing the lane to Gerrans. "Not bad," I murmured complacently. Of Portscatho and the harbour, however, I saw no sign at all. If only I could sight the jetty . . . but wisdom prevailed, and I let go an anchor, which dragged. Drifting a little, I tried again. This time the anchor struck a sandy patch, and the boat came round gently, safe as rocking horse. Since the mist had delayed my arrival by more than half-an-hour, I went below to brew the coffee that I might have missed ashore. Afterwards, while lowering a second anchor, I heard the splash of oars and a familiar voice.

"Is that you, Jacky?" I shouted.

"'Tis me all right," came the reply. "Who the Hell are *you*?"

"*Noah's Ark.*"

"Ah, th'admiral." Jacky stopped rowing. "But what are 'ee doing in this weather?"

"Coming ashore. Am I near the fairway?"

"You'm practically in it. But if you take my advice you'll stay put. 'Tis coming up to high water, and when the tide begins to ebb . . . no, no, you bide on the sand."

By this time the old fisherman and his co-pilot had drifted out of sight, leaving me to sip coffee in a cold miasma, hoping that no other vessel would be rash enough to enter the invisible fairway.

To a deep sea sailor, of course, it would all have seemed child's play, mere amateur pilotage by-God-and-by-guess. Yet the sea is the sea, and the rocks are the rocks, whether in mid-Pacific or within hailing distance of Cornwall. Meantime, since voices carry far across water, I could hear Jacky muttering to his lobster-mate: "Just 'cause they've had a bit o' gold lace on their sleeve they think they can out-sail Saint Columbus. He's not a bad old buffer, though. But I still don't like the way he always uses them bloody charts. I said to'en only last week, 'I've been fishing these waters sixty years,' I said, 'and I don't need no bits o' paper to show me where Portscatho is.' " Nevertheless, Jacky overshot his own moorings, and was heard to say so, in tones that are best described as "nautical".

Ten minutes later I rowed ashore, and there met my friends, who asked why I had failed to arrive on the previous morning.

"Because of the mist," I explained.

"Mist?" They stared incredulously. "But it was glorious weather. The sun shone all day." Then, from their own mist, came an afterthought: "How on earth did you manage to find your way?"

"By the light of the glorious sun," I replied, "which shone until I reached Greeb Point."

Lads of the Land

The farmhand was tedding hay with a pitchfork, whistling because the sun shone. According to the parish register the farm-hand was named Higgs, but according to the national tradition he was named Hodge, a medieval variant of Roger, that time-honoured synonym for the man whom Robert Bridges admired:

> His was ever a life of toil
> In snow and frost, in drought and rain;
> But he is heir and son of the soil,
> And Hodge shall come to his own again.

William Cobbett, a Surrey peasant-farmer, spent most of his long life crusading on behalf of "that class of society that I have always loved and cherished, the people employed in the cultivation of the land." These he dubbed endearingly as "the lads of the land." Their way of life, he said, "gives the best security for health and strength of body ... It necessarily produces early rising; constant forethought; constant attention; constant care of dumb animals." Although it has become a term of abuse, the word "peasant" is an honourable word, connoting the vital role of one who tills the soil of his *pagus* or country. Cobbett himself had no illusions—and very few disillusions—about the English peasantry. He knew that Hodge's narrow outlook went deep. "The nature of all living things," he declared, "are known to country boys better than to philosophers." Wittgenstein might have challenged that proposition, but not even the most logical Positivist will deny Cobbett's claim that, while many townsfolk earn their living by making and selling luxuries, Hodge deals solely in necessities: "His produce," said Cobbett, "consists of things wanted by all mankind."

Some people share Cobbett's belief that country life is an antidote to the myopic envy which bedevils industrial life. Nature, they maintain, teaches men to make a reasonable estimate of sufficiency and then to feel satisfied with it. Fresh air, after all, is better than stale; sunlight outshines desklight; and to plough a field or to thatch a rick is more healthy and less monotonous than to stoke a furnace or to spray a car. There is nothing mystical in the countryman's content; or, rather, mysticism is not a necessary part of it. Few shepherds read Plotinus, and fewer still suffer a Johannine dark night of the soul. Isolated from the grosser examples of what Traherne called "the dirty ways of this world", Hodge was rated simple because he had kept his innocency. As Macaulay observed, even an eighteenth-century squire was cheated by London innkeepers. Toward the middle of that century, however, Hodge saw his ancient pre-eminence threatened by a new form of national economy, which, instead of producing enough food to feed the nation, chose rather to manufacture and export hardware in order to obtain the money with which to buy enough food to feed the nation. Such a lopsided housekeeping could last only for so long as other nations did buy our hardware. Today, having priced ourselves into a spurious prosperity, we find that many of our former customers either manufacture their own hardware or purchase it from non-British markets; yet we continue each year to bury tens of thousands of acres of foodland in a concrete grave.

While Hitler's submarines were bringing Britain to the brink of hunger, H. J. Massingham cried from the wilderness: "the Industrial Revolution and the Enclosures between them demolished the structure and pattern of country life. One thing only can re-people it—the restoration of the peasantry. But that is what industrialism does not understand. Catastrophe alone can teach it to understand." The oil-producing Arabs may not care to be called catastrophic, but they cannot avoid being called catalytic. In 1940 Massingham's dream of a restored peasantry might still have come true albeit modified to suit the substance and the spirit of the age; today the dream is sheer fantasy because one machine performs the work of twelve men, and the men themselves seek higher wages at a factory. Formerly a gregarious occupation, with scores of farmhands working alongside, husbandry is now as lonely as the driver of a weatherproof tractor. Fortunately, not all is yet lost. Farm folk in deep country remain uncorrupted by those evil communications which elsewhere reduce humanity to the lowest and commonest condition of Mammonism. Hodge, indeed, reaps the best of both worlds ... the new sanitation and the old independence, the wider outlook and the deeper roots, the speed of machines and the rhythm of Nature.

At a time when change can scarcely keep pace with itself, the only certainty is uncertainty. Perhaps we shall look to our moat for a marine menu. Perhaps we shall swallow a daily dose of pill-calories. Perhaps grass and plastics will become our *maison's* speciality. Amid all the doubt, however, one fact is indisputable; Hodge wields a power greater than that of any other manual worker. We are unlikely to die from a dearth of coal or of steel or of cars, but if Hodge refused to do his duty, that really would be the last straw, and having eaten it we would starve. The farm and the surgery are the most important servants of mankind. Let us therefore give thanks that Hodge still resists the disease which Hilaire Belloc diagnosed when he said: "Every day there dies some number of those men and women who could remember an England of the countryside and personal loyalties. Soon, very soon, there will be none left but those who, all their lives, have known nothing but the universal wages system of our towns."

The Hills that Spoke

On a winter afternoon in the year 1897 two men were walking slowly to the summit of Doone Beacon. "Shall 'ee make it?" asked the younger man.

"Don't ask damn fool questions," came the reply.

"I only meant ..."

"You meant I'm eighty-eight and ought to be dead."

When at last they reached the summit, they found a group of villagers gathered beside an unlit bonfire. "Blow me down," exclaimed one of the group. "'Tis Granfer Davy. My dear man, you'm past climbing the Beacon, surely?"

"Then how come I've climbed 'en?" retorted the veteran, prodding the faggots with his stick. Then he glanced at the sky. "Another 'alf-hour," he reckoned, "and this yere will be ablaze. Sixty years a Queen, eh? A real diamond jubilee."

"I can remember her silver jubilee," said his companion. "'Twas way back in '62. Lord, Lord, I must be getting older than I thought. Yes," he repeated, "I can remember 1862."

"I," said the old man, "can remember 1815." The group stared, surprised at being astonished by what they had long known. "I walked up yere with my uncle. Least, I walked 'alfway. T'other 'alf I rode on his shoulder. And when we arrived, the faggots were piled just where they are now, and old Jonas standing guard over 'em, same as someone was guarding all the others." He waved his stick. "High Beacon, Windy Point, Gallows Hill, West Tor ... all waiting to be lit in case he landed."

"Napoleon," someone muttered, as though to emphasise the obvious.

"When my uncle was bo'sun in the *Fearless* he'd seen 'em, hundreds of 'em, Boney's barges, lying off the French coast, just waiting till he'd captured the Channel. But he never did. Then as now, we ruled the waves."

"But ..."

"But only just. Terrible short o' ships and men we were. Spending our money on everything except defending our money. 'Twas like the Armada all over again. Some people never seem to learn." He noticed a hamper on the ground. "Do I smell ale?"

"Better be quick about it," his companion warned. "I can see pa'son and the womenfolk coming up. Ah, and there's pa'son's sister."

"That woman?" The old man grabbed a mug. "Her's the most intemperate Temperancer I ever did meet." The ale was swallowed in three quick gulps. "'Tis strange times we'm living in, when a man can't wet the whistle without someone rams a tract down his throat."

So the afternoon faded, growing colder and darker. The parson was already saying: "According to my watch ..." when a shout went up. "There 'tis! Windy Point's afire. Stand back now. Let the vicar see all's done shipshape and Queen's Regulations." Next moment, a red tongue pouted from the faggots, and the flames spread, blotting out the night and the moor and everything except the spectators. Two minutes later and nine miles away, a voice on West Tor cried: "Look! Doone Beacon! Stand by, lads. Now's the time. God save the Queen!"

On a summer evening in the year 1977 an old man and a small boy were walking slowly to the summit of Doone Beacon. "Shall 'ee make it?" asked the greybeard.

"Is it far?" came the reply.

"Far enough to give 'ee another ride. But this time granfer's tired, too, so we'll wait till Dad brings the Land Rover."

"I'm hot, granfer."

"Better that than cold, like I was when I first came up yere. My mother carried me most o' the way."

"Didn't 'er 'ave no Land Rover?"

"The only land roving your great-grandmother ever did was on 'er own two feet, or sometimes with old Jonas in his wagon. Now, let's sit down and see if there's any o' they peppermints left."

Five minutes later the Land Rover appeared, crammed with villagers. "It's long past his bedtime," the child's mother complained.

"Get along with 'ee, girl," said the old man. "This yere's going to be a sight he may never see again. Twenty-five years a Queen. And what years! When they lit the fire for Victoria's jubilee we were the greatest nation in the world. And what are we now?"

"Pack it in, grandpop," said a voice. "This is 1977."

"That's exactly what I was about to say," the old man replied. "But I remember it well, that jubilee. Old Jim Davy climbed up, carrying his eighty-eight years like they were no more than a handful o' pebbles. My mother said afterwards he told 'em about Napoleon's bonfire and all the French barges waiting to invade. We'd not enough ships, said Davy, and not enough men. I reckon 'twas the same as Dunkirk in 1940."

"Did Victoria's bonfire burn good?"

"Bright enough to please Old Nick 'isself. I remember Davy pointing with his stick, counting all the other fires, forty-four on 'em, like red stars from yere to Worcestershire and then across the water to Wales."

Day was a long time dying, but when the last glow from its pyre had faded, a voice shouted: "Look there! Windy's alight."

And a few monents later a voice on West Tor shouted: "They'm firing Doone. Let's give 'em an answer."

So they all stood on their hilltop—men and women and children—counting the myriad fires whose flames were like tongues uttering a grateful salutation: "God save the Queen!"

Green Pastures and Still Waters

The Psalmist saw God as a shepherd: "He maketh me to lie down in green pastures; he leadeth me beside the still waters." The word "still" was not a synonym for "stagnant", but rather an evocation of calm activity. The Prayer Book gives a different translation of those famous words: "He shall ... lead me forth beside the waters of comfort." On a hot summer afternoon it is indeed comforting—because cooling—to stroll beside a river, or simply to sit there, watching sunlight swimming, and reeds nodding, and fish rising, and insects hovering.

Among the world's sizeable islands Britain enjoys an incomparable network of navigable and well-disposed rivers. Sicily, for instance, has no navigable river at all, nor have Iceland, Crete, Corsica, Sardinia. Two thousand years ago the Thames at Lechlade was the port for Cirencester or *Corinium*, the second largest city in Roman Britain. Two hundred years ago, when Defoe reached Lechlade, he found "barges at the key, taking goods for London ..." One hundred years ago the Severn served as commercial highway for West Midland merchandise. Fifty years ago the salt-water Percuil River in Cornwall carried coal to Frooe Farm and other remote households near Gerrans.

Every Briton ought to visit the source of at least one of his rivers. The easiest to find is also the most historic, because the Thames enters our premier city and then flows into what used to be our premier defence, the English Channel, Shakespeare's bulwark,

> Which serves it in the office of a wall,
> Or as a moat defensive to a house,
> Against the envy of less happier lands ...

The source of this famous river can be reached via a footpath at Thames Head Inn on the road from Cirencester to Tetbury. The

landscape is Cotswold with a hint of west country, the Somerset border being less than twenty miles away. Having crossed two or three fields, you arrive at a sylvan hollow, and there—until the 1960s—reclined a statue of Neptune alias Father Thames, erected by the Thames Conservators. The statue now stands at Saint John's Lock, Lechlade, where the lock-keeper can defend it against hooligans. The stream itself is invisible at Thames Head, except after prolonged rain, when the spring breaks and may flood the adjacent land. Above Oxford the river is called Isis; below Oxford it becomes Old Father Thames. Therefore the poet was correct when he said of Thames Head:

> From this, their field, these infant waters run
> Toward the Father that was once a son.

Britain's longest river, the Severn, rises in Montgomeryshire, about two miles north-east of the summit of Plynlimon, whose Celtic name is *Plumlumon Fawr*, though at Llandidloes they spell it according to the day of the week . . . Plinlimmon, Plynlimmon, Pumlymon, and so forth. George Borrow climbed the mountain, and translated the name: "Pum, or Pump, Lummon, signifying the five points, because toward the upper parts, it is divided into five hills . . ." A track through Hafren Forest leads to within half-a-mile of the source, whereafter you must follow the stream uphill to a wooden signboard bearing the words *Source of the Severn*. Some geologists spurn the signboard, arguing that several pools confuse the issue. Borrow, who went there with a guide, felt no such doubts: "The source of the Severn," he stated, "is a little pool of water, some twenty-five inches long, six inches wide, and about three feet deep." Although drought and deluge may modify Borrow's measurements, the general aspect never varies, being perennially level, swampy, treeless, silent; and since the source lies in the centre of a plateau, it grants no glimpse of the other Welsh peaks. Such is the birthplace of Milton's "Sabrina fair." And only a short distance away is the birthplace of the River Wye.

As the Wye rises close to the Severn, so the Exe rises close to the Barle, high in the fastness of Exmoor, not far from The Chains, a near-mountainous swamp, whose overflow caused the flood that swept away part of Lynmouth. Only walkers and horsemen can reach those desolate regions. Leland noted the Barle's seasonal rise and fall: "the water in somer most communely rennith flat upon stones easy to be passid over, but when Raynes cum and storms of Wintre it regith and ys depe." It was on a hot day in August that Richard Jefferies rested beside the Barle, composing a prose paean: "The brown Barle enjoys his life, and splashes in the sunshine like boys bathing—like them he is sunburnt and brown. He laughs and talks, and sings louder than the wind in his woods." So do all rivers when they are young. In the far north, among the solitudes of Caithness, the Forsinard Burn resembles a miniature Niagara, hurling its rainbowed spray across the lonely lane. Even the leisurely Avon hurries from its source in a Northamptonshire garden.

But rivers need not be dramatic in order to seem delightful. The mere sight of water is a kind of slaking; and if the water comes from a mountain beck it will to some palates taste better than wine: *in vino vitaque*. Any river that you love, whether it be long or short, famous or obscure ... the lazy-winding Stour at Halford in Warwickshire, the meditative Nene at Fotheringhay in Northamptonshire, the blue-eyed Lune at Kirkby Lonsdale in Westmorland, the Little Ouse at Willen in Buckinghamshire, Walter Scott's bonnie Tweed at Abbotsford in Roxburghshire, Rupert Brooke's willowy Granta in Cambridgeshire, Andrew Lang's headlong Windrush in Oxfordshire, Izaak Walton's fishable Dove in Derbyshire, Wordsworth's Duddon in Lakeland, Herrick's Dart in Devon, Jerome's Isis in Berkshire ... each is shaded by trees, and serenaded by birds. Along them you may stroll, beside them you may sit, watching men make hay while the sun shines.

7

The Middle Watch

Lamplight from the portholes carved yellow circles on the water, vivid as huge primroses that opened and closed in rhythm with a gentle swell. Astern, the Saint Anthony Lighthouse ploughed a white furrow on a black field, and was answered by the Lizard light sweeping its metronomic fan across the sky. Far ahead, the village identified itself via a galaxy of lamplit windows from harbour to hilltop.

With a square yard of canvas as mizzen-cum-sheet-anchor, *Noah's Ark* drifted through moonlight, apparently motionless until an unbroken wave slapped the clinker hull, swaying an oilskin on its peg. Another motionless minute elapsed, followed by another surge, which this time heaved the screw out of the water, so that the bilges gurgled, and a mug of cocoa dribbled on the combing.

Half-a-mile to seaward a yacht came full-sail, stately as Andrew Young's vision:

> How lovely are these swans
> That float like high proud galleons . . .

Presently the yacht altered course and then hove-to before making the final run into Helford River. I could just hear the clatter of her lowered sails and a throb as the engine came to life. Then her masthead light moved forward like a golden star against the silver constellations.

When I went below, the clock said midnight or Middle Watch; the barometer was poised between Fair and Very Dry; the dog slept on his locket seat. Utter peace prevailed, the only man-made sound being a simmer from the stove. And there I sat, in a glow of gentle light in a world of creaking sibilance, less than two miles from telephones and transistors, yet feeling as though I were a day's voyage from the nearest inhabited island. All the same, a sailor is trained to be perpetually on watch. Even while relaxing, he reckons how far he has drifted, how soon he must

resume course, how swiftly another vessel may have appeared on the empty horizon. In wartime he learns to sleep through much clanging, but when the engines stop unexpectedly, he wakes and wonders.

After a while I chugged home at six silvery knots which grew creamy where the bow churned the starry surface. Passing through a shaft of the Saint Anthony Light, I felt like a fugitive escaping from a Socialist Republic. In the Saint Mawes fairway the water was dead calm, encompassed by hills. Past Percuil I went, the creek narrowing while the hills climbed. Then the throttle closed, the anchor dived, the dinghy bumped, and for several moments the universe seemed to echo the sound of my movement, stowing the sail, lashing the painter, filling the kettle. That done, I rowed the dog ashore; and again we sounded loud, creaking the rowlocks, splashing the water, crunching the shingle. Viewed from a distance, *Noah's Ark* resembled Thomas Hardy's moonlit vessel:

> In a solitude of the sea
> Deep from human vanity . . .

At about one o'clock, having put the boat to bed, I leaned against the wheel. On each side of the creek the hills etched their own dark horizon, and the stars admired themselves Narcissus-like in the water. Luminous seaweed glided past, quieter than silence, delicate as lace. Once or twice a token breeze ruffled the tide, and then the lace indulged a series of tiny switchbacks; but chiefly it flowed like laundered linen. Whenever I moved, the boat's slight motion sent ripples that set the stars leaping in their looking glass. Once, an owl hooted, as though calling for an even deeper stillness.

There are not many occasions when you can stand motionless in English moonlight without soon feeling cold; to do so on salt water is indeed exceptional. At such an hour on such a night you measure the moon's slow abdication, or, if you prefer, the Earth's nocturnal arc. At three o'clock I turned-in, lulled nine-tenths asleep by the loveliness of the night and the activity of the day. Midway between sleeping and waking I heard a lark, and with one drowsy eye observed that the turning tide had swivelled the boat broadside-on, so that the starboard portholes faced toward the east, revealing a patch of pale grey which gradually turned pink. Then a cuckoo called, bouncing his reveille round the creek.

One part of me wished to sleep, but another part noticed a circle of daylight shimmering like a halo on the cabin roof. Which, then, should triumph . . . light, or dark? Yesterday, or today? The dog settled the matter, jumping from the locker to the deck and thence into the cockpit, and from the cockpit up to the combing, and from the combing down to the dinghy, which he had long ago assumed as his own command. Shamed into action, I took a customary morning bath; that is, I pinched my nostrils and then stepped over the side. On re-entering the cabin, I heard a dinghy being dragged across the sand, and after that a voice over the water: *"Noah's Ark,* you'm showing an early leg."

Peering through the porthole, I shouted: "Chief, you're turning-in late."

"Late?" The retired yeoman-of-signals fell silent, his own signal having been trumped. So, in rising sunlight, I lit the stove, boiled an egg, and ate it on deck while the warmth grew warmer.

At noon I decided to take a short nap, but it lasted so long that on waking I found the boat high and dry in the mud, with a full hour to go before the tide would set her on an even keel.

Jack the Russell

My Lakeland terrier belongs to that select company of dogs who come within sight of their seventeenth year. Although his eyes and ears have lost much of their keenness, he still ambles round the paddocks, still eats well, sleeps well, and presumably feels well. Only last month the vet pronounced him free of any complaint except age. Even so, the end cannot be far off, and I must soon suffer the non-response which Thomas Hardy received from his own departed friend:

> Should you call as when I knew you,
> I shall not turn to view you,
> I shall not listen to you,
> Shall not come.

In order to soften the inevitable blow, I lately acquired an eight-weeks-old Jack Russell.

Some people deny that a Jack Russell breed exists. At most they allow a hybrid strain of dumpy terrier, unofficially classified as an Exmoor terrier. Why, then, are the dogs called Jack Russells? By way of genealogical answer, we find that in 1795 a certain John Russell, son of an Anglican parson, was born at Dartmouth in Devonshire, and that while still a schoolboy at Blundells he mastered his own pack of beagles (two-and-a-half couple). As an

Oxford undergraduate he not only followed three packs of fox-hounds but also bred his own terriers. Having been ordained deacon, Russell served as curate at South Molton, on the edge of Exmoor, where he met and married the daughter of Admiral Bury, who lived nearby at Swimbridge. Since Mrs Russell's cousin held the advowson of Swimbridge, John Russell ultimately became vicar of that parish and master of his own foxhounds. When he was eighty-four years old he mastered yet another pack, with which, in his eighty-sixth year, he fell while jumping. After lying speechless for an hour, he suddenly recovered his voice, called for his horse, and rode home.

The sparse evidence suggests that Russell's hunt terriers did resemble those which now perpetuate his name; but their origin remains a mystery. The most likely of several conflicting accounts runs as follows: when Russell was an undergraduate he took a fancy to a terrier belonging to the milkman at Marston, which he crossed with one of his own bitches. Later in life he crossed his bitches with a terrier either from the Quorn or from the Grove (the evidence on that point is vague). Such, in brief, was the genesis of Jack Russells.

Now everyone believes that their own dog is a paragon of intelligence, fortitude, affection, and whatever other merit a man attributes to his faithful fellow-traveller through this vale of tears. My own puppy—now slowly learning to answer to the name of Jack—is rough-haired and completely white, except for a fawn or lemon-coloured face. Like all the best country dogs, he is learning to sleep in a kennel in a shed adjoining the house, where he has already accumulated a number of treasures, chief among them being my second-best cardigan. He shows little interest in any object unless it is either vastly larger or immensely smaller than himself. Ants, for example, arouse intense curiosity, and a fallen tree becomes a challenge to a tug-of-war. At present he has barked once only, when the sound of his own voice so terrified him that he ran away, as though to disassociate himself from the sound. He made friends with Shap, the Lakeland, at their very first sniff; and it is a pretty sight to watch the old warrior patiently accepting the assaults and sallies of his pert companion. Like the biblical lion and lamb, the two dogs lie down together, each in a corner of the veteran's basket. Unlike Shap, however, the newcomer has not yet canonised himself.

G

The casualty list to date includes one rose bush, two antirrhinums, five sweet williams, most of this morning's postbag, and the aforesaid cardigan. I have also to report that one gum boot is missing and must be presumed lost (an absent dustpan was found in the wood).

When Jack first arrived, the ginger cat reserved judgement, but after two days he decided in favour of the plaintive puppy. It is quite remarkable to observe the way in which Ginger retracts his claws while administering a playful tap. If the puppy becomes too skittish, the cat hisses, and the hint is taken, for the semantics of animal psychology are simple and stark, a fact which Gilbert White stated succinctly: "little is said, but much is meant and understood." To have buried three generations of long-lived dogs is to become acutely conscious of your own mortality. Nearly sixty years ago, perhaps, you were given your first puppy. Then followed those loving companions of your adolescence, your marriage, your decades of professional achievement; and always you survived the well-remembered friends. But a time comes when you find yourself wondering whether the new puppy will one day outwalk his master. If Jack the Russell lives as long as Shap the Lakeland, then his master will need to be a very old gentleman indeed if they are both to amble round the paddocks in their dotage.

Meanwhile, the puppy thrives on his native moorland air, and will, we trust, enjoy many memorable experiences ... his first ascent of Dunkery Beacon and a view of the Welsh hills across the Severn Sea; his first taste of the Atlantic at Woolacombe; his first sight of a stag among the heather at Prayway; his first squelch on the marshy Chains above Lynmouth; his first gallop across Shap Fell, the Westmorland home of his old kennel mate. Already his diary shows a winter sojourn at Land's End, a spring pilgrimage to John o' Groats, a summer appearance in the Quantocks, and (at the end of this month) a finger-crossed introduction to the new rug in front of the fire.

Reaping the Whirlwind

A grey pall crept across the sky, moving slowly from the south-west. Nothing else seemed to move at all. Every leaf appeared

to be glued to its twig. The corn stood motionless. The cattle were supine in shade. Lit by a dwindling gap of blue sky, the grass assumed an unnatural brightness. Then the pall closed the gap, and the brightness changed to gloom. Midges disappeared. Flowers contracted. The silence was uncanny.

Presently the pall darkened and became oppressively low, edged with black, like an old-fashioned mourning card. After that a breeze got up, rustling the silence, shimmering the corn, stroking the grass. Aware of the impending storm, sheep moved from mid-meadow to the lee of a linhay while one bee raced down the lane, ignoring the succulent foxgloves. Two minutes later the breeze died away, leaving the air more than ever stifling, and the silence more than ever eerie. Villagers shut their windows, hurriedly dragging deck chairs indoors. Harvesters glanced at the black clouds and then at the uncut corn. The farmer shouted: "Come on, lads. Jump to it. Let's save what we can."

Some people still suppose that thunderstorms are the result of a collision between clouds, a fallacy propagated two thousand years ago by Lucretius in his atomic epic, *De Rerum Natura*. "The reason why the blue expanses of Heaven are shaken by thunder," he declared, "is the clashing of clouds soaring in the atmosphere, when conflicting winds cause them to collide." Thanks partly to Benjamin Franklin's highflying kites, we now know that summer storms usually occur when a heat wave is overtaken by a layer of cold air which causes the warm air to rise and form raindrops. This moisture alternately coalesces and splits, generating a positive charge of electricity in itself and a negative charge in the surrounding atmosphere. Positive charges may multiply until a cloud unleashes millions of volts. Although few folk are killed by British thunderstorms, a number are injured, some of whom court disaster by brandishing metal golf clubs from exposed positions on a hill. Others ask for trouble by sheltering under a corrugated iron roof. Intelligent countrymen, on the other hand, go to earth in a ditch or under a low hedge. While waiting for the storm to pass, they compute its progress. If, for example, the flash and the clap are registered instantly, and if the latter is heard five seconds after the former is seen, then the storm-centre is approximately a mile away. If, however, the clap and the flash are registered simultaneously, then the observer will probably lose interest in anything except his own survival.

In describing a thunderstorm, music and painting have an advantage over poetry and prose, for a painter can depict lightning exactly as we see it, and a composer can translate thunder more or less as we hear it (no one has excelled the verisimilitude of the storm in Beethoven's Pastoral Symphony). James Thompson's thunderstorm was a very Augustan spectacle:

> At first, heard solemn o'er the verge of heaven,
> The tempest growls.

After the growl, the roar:

> . . . as it nearer comes,
> And rolls the awful burden on the wind,
> The lightnings flash a larger course, and more
> The noise astounds . . .

After the roar, the rain:

> Down comes the deluge of sonorous hail,
> Or prone-descending rain. Wide-rent, the clouds
> Pour a whole deluge . . .

When a storm does break, it seems to echo Edmund Spenser's question: "And is there care in heaven?" Men and beasts alike are awed by the crashing peals and the lethal forks. Gunfire and contrived explosions they can understand because such things are purposeful and controllable, but thunder and lightning have no purpose, unless to be the inevitable effects of an uncontrollable cause. The damage caused by violent thunderstorms is far greater than the benefit conferred by the minerals which they release from the atmosphere. A farmer's year-long labour can be laid low and worthless by a storm that flattens the standing wheat. In spring a prolonged deluge can wash away the new-drilled seed. When Pliny wrote of *brutum fulmen* or "a senseless thunderbolt" his adjective meant "harmless" rather than "aimless". Our forefathers, however, saw the lightning as very purposeful indeed, for it was a message from the gods, and it did not bring reassurance. On the contrary, it caused men to remember their sins: "they have sown the whirlwind," cried Hosea, "and shall reap the whirlwind." Something of that primitive terror still lingers. Centuries of sophisticated *hubris* are ripped away while the storm sizzles and rumbles. Then indeed the old gods rise wrathful from a racial Unconscious, and the Shibboleths of science seem puny and irrelevant, powerless either to curb or to quell the terrifying drama. "And a great and strong wind rent the mountains, and brake in pieces the rocks . . . and after the wind an earthquake . . . and after the earthquake a fire . . . and after the fire a still small voice." Although the Bible's poetic prose has fallen from favour, never to be revived by a generation that talks like a telephone, the "still small voice" continues to speak when the storm has passed. Hearing it, the air grows cool, the sky turns blue, the grass gleams, the birds sing, and the flowers hold their heads high, like men who have slaked a great thirst.

A Countryman in London

I come up to London twice a year, chiefly in order to visit my dentist. Nine times out of ten I reach Paddington about half-an-hour before the appointment begins, and return thither about half-an-hour after the appointment has ended. London and I get along very well without each other.

On the rare and reluctant occasions when I am compelled to remain in town for most of the day, I follow a route that was taken by Charles Lamb when he praised the quasi-rustic quietude of the lawyers' Temple beside the Thames: "What a transition for a countryman visiting London . . . the passing from the crowded Strand or Fleet street, by unexpected avenues, into its magnificent ample square, its classic green recesses!" Fleet Street and the Strand are probably more crowded and certainly more thunderous than in Lamb's day, but the din enhances rather than diminishes the collegiate calm of a legal Elysium whose circular Temple Church was founded by the Knights Templars, consecrated by the Patriarch of Jerusalem in 1185, and re-dedicated in 1958, having survived the blitz. The Knights themselves, however, became too powerful, and were dispossessed of their estate, which ultimately passed to the lawyers of the Inner and Middle Temples, who built their own residential quarters.

No one in Fleet Street ever looks for a blade of grass, nor listens for a singing bird. Such irrelevances belong to a distant *terra incognita*. In the Temple Gardens, by contrast, even a countryman feels that milk and wheat might be culled from the soil. Beyond the precincts—only a few hundred yards away—the world throbs with Lamb's "quick pulse of gain," but within the precincts life moves leisurely. Here are the junior barristers . . . black coats and pinstripe trousers . . . carrying their wig and gown in a blue bag; here, too, the seniors, carrying their accoutrements in a red bag. Here come plaintiffs, defendants, witnesses, wards; here also the solicitors who usher those agitated litigants. Sometimes a judge walks past, carrying, as it were, a man's life, or a woman's reputation, or a company's assets. As for the clerks, they carry brief cases that really do contain briefs.

Once or twice during my perambulations I meet an old Oxford crony . . . erudite H., for example, who, in the years when I rowed bow, uttered from the second thwart such grunts and imprecations as would have silenced Judge Jeffreys himself. Then there is lordly M., who seldom pleads nowadays, but remains in his chambers, offering counsel's opinion. What a forthright welcome he accords me: "Ah, a breath of country air!" I fancy that the "country air" is a synonym for the tang of Harris tweed, since I never dress formally unless on formal occasions.

In the Temple Gardens a countryman no longer feels beset by concrete and commerce and cacophony. Green grass, after all, looks much the same, the world over. Trees are as comely in London as in Lakeland. And if the Temple sparrows look less spruce than their Exmoor cousins, that is an environmental misfortune, not an innate fault. I have never heard a cuckoo in the gardens, but blackbirds are common, and I once thought I saw a stonechat (ornithologists tell me it was possible though unlikely).

This urban rusticity spans the four seasons. In spring the murky river and the dusty trees sparkle, as though responding to Laurence Binyon's evocation of the Thames above Eynsham:

> To his old shores the river
> A new song was singing,
> And young shoots were springing
> On old roots for ever.

In summer, while London wilts under a brash sky, the Temple Gardens create a shaded oasis. In autumn the leaf-littered lawns remind one of the Fellows' garden at Merton, or the gated vista at Trinity. On winter nights, when "the busy world is hushed, and the fever of life is over," the barristers' work is by no means done. As in an Oxford college, lamplit windows warm the darkness while a chink in the curtains reveals a pile of leatherbound volumes, and a cluster of pink-ribboned documents, and a halo of studious pipe smoke. Those academic associations are emphasised whenever a carillon is heard, which during the day was drowned by traffic. The great bell of Saint Paul's tolls the hour, the Middle Temple answers, Saint Clement Danes juggles its Oranges and Lemons, and Big Ben sets a sonorous seal on the chorus.

Day or night, winter or summer, the Temple is numinous. Here Shakespeare's *Twelfth Night* received its première. Here the Benchers dined Sir Francis Drake, who presented them with the lamp which had lit his cabin in the *Golden Hind* (when that ship was broken up the Benchers made a wine table of her timbers). Here sat a youth named Charles Dickens, taking shorthand notes (with future reference to Messrs. Dobson and Fogg). Here, as a Bencher of the Middle Temple, the Queen Mother dines on high occasions. Here, in these dusty chambers, drank and devilled and dreamed the juniors who became Lord High Chancellor, Lord Chief Justice, Attorney-General, Governor-General. Here are wooden stairways creaking to rooms that survived the Great Fire of 1666. Here are law and order, equity and punishment, tradition and innovation, modern precedent and the ageless clash of human interests.

Lamb stated a fact when he described the Temple as "the most elegant spot in the metropolis."

8

A Night on the Tiles

The animals were so valuable that Ifor, as head stockman, was
sent to accompany them on their journey to the London Docks.
"The trip will do him good," Sir Robert said. "It's high time he
saw a bit of the world." Ifor himself, who was past seventy years
old, obeyed with some misgiving, torn between care for a herd
which he had helped to build, and reluctance to forsake his
native mountains, which he had left only once before, to attend
a grandson's wedding at Shrewsbury.

Having delivered the animals to an agent on the quay, Ifor
followed his next instructions by taking a cab to a hotel in the
West End, a large and impersonal establishment, much favoured
by birds of passage. "Your bill has been paid," Sir Robert had
assured him, "and we've reserved a seat for you on the train.
Get to Paddington at noon, and take things slowly."

It was an early evening when Ifor reached the hotel. A fierce
sun scorched the pavements and the hordes scurrying thereon.
Ifor's suitcase—a green canvas one—was taken from him by a
commissionaire. "Dressed like an admiral," was Ifor's comment
when he returned home, and described his adventures. Meanwhile,
he wiped his boots on a mat marked *Grand de Luxe*, tiptoed to the
reception desk, then to the lift, and finally along an endlessly
carpeted corridor. "Like a rich man's prison it was, and every cell
with the number written copperplate in gold ink. Mine was
seventy-seven." Having washed his hands, Ifor lit a pipe, and
after an involuntary exploration of the entire premises found
his way to the restaurant. "In London," he told Dai, "if you want

beef you must ask for berf. Foreign, I suppose, or else they can't pronounce their own language." After the beef, he was asked what he would like to follow. Forgetting the march of events, he replied: "I'll have some of Mam's sago." There was none left, they told him. "So they brought me a slice of cake instead. Called it ghetto or somesuch. It was nice enough, mind. The sort of thing Mam bakes for the Temperance Mothers. They said quite a lot of people nowadays were switching from cocoa to coffee, so I did the same. But the cup was that small I wouldn't have offered it to a tadpole."

After dinner Ifor stood on the kerb outside the hotel, waiting for the traffic to give way. When his patience became exhausted he stepped into the street, and was near-missed by a bus. Alone on the narrow island, he flinched while the cars roared past.

After several minutes he regained the safety of the hotel, and went up to his room, feeling shaken. Number seventy-seven was unbearably hot, so he opened a window, and peered down on the hive of swarming London. The din struck him like a physical blow. He took a deep breath, trying to taste clean air. "By this time it was a quarter-to-ten, and everywhere people. I said to myself, 'Don't they need to wake up tomorrow? Have they no work?'"

After two sleepless and stifling hours he got out of bed, and once more peered down. "Dammit, the people were still there. Black ones and white ones and brown ones ... I saw one chap strolling around with his shirt-tail hanging out, and coloured flowers painted all over it. Mam would have tucked it in pretty quick, that's for sure."

At two in the morning, still sleepless and gasping for breath, Ifor could endure it no longer. He therefore dressed and then walked down the corridor, where he found a door marked *Escape*. "That's the way for me," he muttered. The door opened to a flight of steel stairs leading to the roof; and there he remained. "They were singing and shouting in the street, and someone being sick by the sound of it. But I still couldn't breath, though. Not properly. And never a blade of grass anywhere."

After what seemed an eternity he became conscious of something that really was familiar, for out of the east arose the faint lessening of darkness which is the birth of dawn. Somewhere a sparrow chirped; somewhere else a lark leaped up, loud as a glad reveille. A great longing came over Ifor, such as he had not experienced for many years. Still with the birdsong echoing through his brain, he returned to number seventy-seven, packed the green canvas suitcase, and tiptoed to the lift, which twice arrived at an even higher storey. However, he managed to find the escape route again, and eventually reached a small court-yard, where several packing cases enabled him to climb over the wall.

He had no precise plan, nor even a vague one. He wished only to be home. He wished to hear Mam's voice: "Six o'clock, bach. Time to be stirring!" He wished to hear the stream singing and the hens clucking. He wished to see the walls of Maesllan, white-washed and shining in the sun. He wished to see Moel Fawr, tall as a green spire above a grey mist. At that moment a taxi appeared.

Ifor waved his suitcase. "Paddington!" he shouted. "Quick as you like." But he need not have hurried, because he arrived too late for the last train and too early for the first.

Several hours later he stepped onto his native soil; and half-an-hour after that, Dai the grocer delivered him at the crossroads. When the van had disappeared, Ifor took a gulp of real air. Not one bird, but a whole skyful, sang a welcome. Moel Fawr rose up, bright as a sun-tipped sceptre. And the track to Maesllan was a white ribbon on a green sea. Ifor removed his jacket, loosened his crumpled tie, and entered paradise, singing "Glorious things of thee are spoken . . ."

Mam heard him while she was milking Lilac in the byre. "Ifor?" She could scarcely believe it. "At this hour? But we weren't expecting you till teatime earliest. In fact, Sir Robert said if you missed the midday train . . ." She paused, peering at the silver stubble, the crumpled tie, the sleepy eyes. "It is tired you look. Have you been spending a night on the tiles?"

The Finest View in Britain

Where is the finest view in Britain? Questions of that sort evoke a lively response. Moreover, the liveliness will contain some surprises because "finest" is often a synonym for "best-loved", as, for example, the view from Hotley Lane on the edge of Prestwood in the Buckinghamshire Chilterns.

If you descend a few yards from the summit of that lane you will notice a cottage beside a cart track on your left, and if you follow that track you will notice another cottage on your left, and if you look to your right you will see a meadow which slopes so steeply that it hides the farmhouse in a valley whence the fields climb to a summit of beechwoods stretching left and right, far as the eye can see. Two-thirds of the way up, overlooking a No Through Road, stands one of the smallest churches in Britain, a whitewashed medieval church with a timber Tudor porch. Westward the hills sweep out of sight, and are crowned by an even higher hill which creates an impression of distance enhanced by mystery. All in all, the view combines intimacy and spacious-ness, height and depth, woods and pastures, solitude and companionship; and the same may be said of thousands of other views in Britain. But I own myself partial because for thirty-five years I saw the view whenever I glanced up from my desk.

Impatient Scots are waiting for me to praise Ben Nevis, the roof of Britain, more than four thousand feet above the sea. For perhaps six days in each year the Ben offers maximum visibility, scanning its native land and far beyond, even to the Irish coast. But you do not need to reach the summit in order to gain an impression of height. A few hundred yards short of the top is a narrow ledge, from which you peer down dizzily at a much lower ledge, from which—an hour earlier—you had dizzily peered down at a hostel in the foothills.

"One of the loveliest scenes in England" . . . so says a plaque on the churchyard wall above the River Lune at Kirkby Lonsdale in Westmorland. That testimony, by the way, came from a connoisseur of beauty, John Ruskin. Here, then, is the Prestwood view writ large, with a river to water it, and across the river a surge of green pasture toiling to the brow of Barbon Fell.

And so it goes on, the lucky dip from which your own choice has a million-to-one-chance of emerging . . . the view of Lynmouth Harbour, deep as the waves, and over it Lynton, high as an eagle, seen from Countisbury in Devon; the view of Stroma, snowcapped under a blue sky, seen from John o' Groats in Caithness; the woods around Battle, site of the Battle of Hastings, seen from Netherfield in Sussex; Bodmin Moor, stony and many-tracked, seen from Brown Willy, Cornwall's apex; Dunkery Beacon, the pinnacle of Exmoor, seen from the Brendon Hills in Somerset; Golden Cap and the English Channel, blazoned vert on a field azure, seen from the hills above Shipton Gorge in Dorset; the Eden Valley and the Lakeland peaks, jagged as the ramparts of a ruined city, seen from Cross Fell in Cumberland; Housman's "coloured counties" and Quiller-Couch's "pastoral heart of England," seen at sunrise from Bredon Hill in Worcestershire. And still it goes on . . . Scotland and the Isle of Man, seen from Slieve Donard, nearly three thousand feet above the sea that laps the edge of Ulster's Mourne Mountains; the Long Mynd, seen from the Roman Watling Street near Church Stretton in Shropshire; the Quantocks, birthplace of *Lyrical Ballads*, seen from the Beacon at Malvern in Worcestershire; Tan Hill Inn, England's loftiest, seen from the Pennine Way near Hawes in

Yorkshire; the Roman lighthouse, crowning the white cliffs of Dover, seen from a ship in the Channel; The Cheviot, Northumberland's highest point, seen from the lane near Ingram; the summit of Snowdon, almost as majestic as the view therefrom, seen near the precipice at Clogwyn du'r Arddu; the Cotswolds, carved like a blue and static wave, seen from the Ridgeway above Inkpen in Berkshire. There indeed are Marlowe's

> hills and valleys, dale and field
> And all the craggy mountains . . .

The race, however, is not always to the distant nor yet to the lofty. If, for example, you enter the Fens near Spalding you will find a lane—indeed, you may find a dozen lanes—from which, when you lie down in the sun, nothing is visible except the ears of golden corn swaying beside the verge. When you peer above the corn, still you see only more corn, equally golden and likewise swaying; but when your eyes have adjusted themselves to the glare, you notice a farmhouse marooned in an ocean of corn (and if you approach the house you will probably discover that the track leading to it is flanked hip-high by the harvest).

Where, indeed, is Britain's finest view? Rural sentiments must not be allowed to contradict urban facts. When Wordsworth stood on Westminster Bridge he said simply:

> Earth has not anything to show more fair . . .

Again, if you venture into one of the alleyways near the summit of Highgate Hill you will look down on a panorama of London . . . secular towers, ecclesiastical steeples, commercial chimneys, residential roofs. Nor is that all, for in clear weather you will sight the Kentish hills and the pageant which impressed Defoe: "A view over the whole vale, to the city," he wrote. "And that so eminently that they see the very ships passing up and down the river for 12 or 15 miles below London."

If you venture further into bricks and mortar—say, among the back streets of Manchester and Glasgow—you will meet people who, when they return from their holiday at Clacton or in Corsica, glance round at the mean houses, the omnipresent gasworks, the derelict canal, and with a sigh of relief murmur: "Eh, but it's good to be home."

Harvest Home

The hill on which this house stands is in many respects a replica of Traherne's:

> The way at first is rough and steep,
> And something hard for to ascend;
> But on the top do pleasures keep
> And ease and joys do still attend.

By crossing a meadow I reach a point from which the Dartmoor mountains are visible, and the Exmoor peaks so close that sheep are seen grazing the heather. Since the summit lies within three minutes' walk, it offers a happy hunting ground to the dog, now one year old and therefore blessed with effervescent energy.

On our latest ascent I came to a lane that meanders along the spine of the hill, and there I leaned against a gate overlooking Exmoor. As a rule I tend to ignore the foreground and to gaze at the lofty hinterland, nearly two thousand feet high. This time, however, I became aware of looking at a portrait framed by the gate and the trees. The background was still visible, of course, but it had been overshadowed by the near and middle distances, which were a mass of corn, stooked in the old style, each golden clutch slanting like a steeply-thatched roof. It made a picture not easily forgotten, nor likely to be forgotten in an age when machines strew the stubble with prepacked bales. But was the picture really outstanding? Or had the ancient methods of husbandry added a sentimental lustre to a seasonal ritual? I looked again, and decided beyond doubt that all occasions were indeed conspiring to create a scene of exceptional beauty. For one thing, the atmosphere was pellucid despite the heat. For another, the breeze was just brisk enough to stir the leaves. Chiff-chaffs recited their miniature litany, and larks formed a festival choir. In short, the stooks and the stubble blended with clouds and sunlight to paint a picture vivid as any that Cézanne found at Aix-le-Provence.

From a field below the brow a tractor started up, so I walked toward it, and saw that the corn in one part of the field was still uncut, its tall stalks swaying as though in rhythm with Traherne's

cadence: "The corn was orient and immortal wheat, which never should be reaped, nor was ever sown. I thought it had stood from everlasting to everlasting." This corn, however, was not immortal, for the harvesters were already climbing the hill; nor had the corn stood *ab initio*, for I had watched the ploughing of its seedbed and the harrowing of its tilth. How distant those dark days seemed; how remote the rain and the mist and the teatime lamplight. Even the later days were dim ... those cuckoo-dawns in April, those rosebud sunsets in May. And now, once again, another year had waned.

"The harvest is past," sighed Jeremiah, "the summer ended ..." But Job faced the autumn with equanimity: "Thou shalt come down to thy grave at a full age, like as a shock of corn cometh in his season." Technology has not outdated the staff of life, on whose strength Jacob leaned when he said to his sons: "Behold, I have heard that there is corn in Egypt: get you down thither, and buy for us from thence; that we may live, and not die."

My thoughts went back to another parched summer and to the farmer who tempered his *Confitebor tibi* with a respectful admonition: "I marvel we'm reaping at all. The soil is like pepper. 'Twasn't all that while ago I said, 'We'll not need a reaper this year. What we'll need is a plough, and then start all over again.' But there it is. God always sends us something in the end. I do truly wish, though, He wouldn't wrap His blessings in such zany weather. 'Tis as though He'd no knowledge of farming. No knowledge at all. That's what I find so puzzling. But there it is. I'll just about cover my costs. Leastways I won't have to pay no income tax to subsidise somebody's strike picket."

The three harvesters were in sight now, shirt-sleeved and thirsty as they halted to swig cider from a whisky bottle. The farmer and the tractor driver, being elderly, wore shirts, but the youngster was stripped to his waist. As they drew near I overheard the veterans discussing a bygone harvest. "Must ha' been 1921 since we suffered such a teetotal September. I remember it well. Not a sign o' rain from Rogation to Michaelmas. And when at last the corn really was ripe, blow me down if the rain didn't start, and th'old farmer ... a reg'lar Methody ... he yelled out, 'Strong drink is a mocker. You'm not touching a drop o' my cider till the last stook is gathered.' And by golly we didn't. But th'old fella made up for it when he give us an 'arvest supper. 'Men,' he said, 'don't never breathe a word o' this to the elders o' the chapel, but in those two casks,' he said, 'there's enough cider to get 'ee pissed for a twelvemonth.' Reuben he was called. Reuben Buckland. Lived to be ninety did old Reub. And his last words were, 'Call me five o'clock tomorrow morning.' So they did. But he never answered 'cause he'd risen earlier than expected."

Then the reaper went into action, and the blades whirled, and the corn fell, and the sun shone, and the men stooked. And when

H

they had gone home to supper, the moon came up, vast as a cosmic orange; and a rabbit crinkled through the stubble, and an owl hooted from the coppice, and the good earth slept among the sheaves.

Hands Across the Sea

Our little country town was in festive mood, decked with British Union Jacks and French Tricolours, all waving *bienvenue* to visitors from the newly-twinned town across the Channel or, as the French call it, *La Manche*, the "Sleeve". During the previous week a party of French boys and girls had arrived, and now the borough was extending a more formal welcome to their elders who would ratify the rustic *entente cordiale*.

It was an eighteenth-century Frenchman who dismissed the English as "a nation of shopkeepers." Our twentieth-century French guests certainly allowed that we had not lost our flair for window-dressing. Thus, the boutique achieved a bravura of frocks, handbags, and scarves in various patterns of red and white and blue. The staid Gents Outfitter displayed tricolour shorts, tricolour socks, and braces to match. No shop was so small, nor any so sequestered, that it did not wave a welcome to the Gauls. Soapflakes and mutton chops, lamp shades and fishing rods, linseed and linoleum, tea trays and gum boots ... all were arrayed against a three-coloured background; and the closer you looked the more you admired. Dustbins, for example, are not usually associated with lyricism; yet there they stood, like three plump and headless Britannias, each flaunting a tricolour sash. Only the undertaker maintained a monochromatic Business as Usual.

Older townsfolk, who remembered the years when Britain was Great, stood outside the Market Hall, stolidly surveying the heirs of an enemy whom their ancestors had trounced at Crécy, Agincourt, Ramillies, Malplaquet, Blenheim, Trafalgar, Waterloo. These veterans—gaitered, breeched, capped—were the last of the John Bulls, the men whom Lamb saluted as "Frank, plain, and English all over." With cheeks as tanned as his leggings, one farmer spoke for many: "I've nothing against 'em, mind. Nothing at all. In fact, they'm very welcome ... ah, and a sight better behaved than some of our own youngsters at Barnstaple. Even so, we'm Devon yereabouts, and we'm not ashamed of it. I've no patience with this modern notion that a Zulu is the same as a Heskimo. For one thing, I can't understand a bloody word they'm saying. And the way they wave their hands about, you'd think they'd got Saint Vitus." Another veteran had visited the French town in 1916: "We lost half our battalion there. Still, the Frenchies were proper friendly. I remember a girl called Colette ..." he halted, glancing at his wife. "It was a long time ago. I had some hair then, and all my teeth."

Resplendent in tricolour headscarf, an Exmoor housewife asserted her affinity with France: "My eldest and me we learned to speak from a gramophone record. Real good we was. When we got off the boat at Boolong a jondarm nudged me, so I said to 'en, 'Vooze ate un un, nate vooze par?' Did he what? Understand? My dear soul, he understood all right. In fact, he thanked God for the English. 'Laze Onglaze,' he said. 'Ah, mon dew!' "

It was good to see young Devonians strolling arm-in-arm with young Bretons: good also to see their elders likewise linked; each rooted in their native soil, but no longer believing that any one nation was inherently superior to all the rest. As for the monoglot farmer, he stuck to his defensive guns, comparing the gesticulated "Mais certainement" with the phlegmatic "Okay by me." Had he spoken French, he would have discovered that many of the Bretons knew more about English history than did many of their English hosts.

The programme of festivities showed that the five gala days included a cycle race, a football match, a fancy dress ball, and an "Entertainment organised by the High Temperature Engineering Co. in the Pannier Market." The English way of life appeared as "Bingo organised by Mr W. Webber, Old Assembly Rooms." Music was free ("The Town Band will march up the field and play before kick-off"), but food had to be paid for ("Ram Roast, Hot Dog Stall, Refreshments and Beer Tent"). On the final day, amid brilliant sunshine, our lady mayor and her wigged town clerk mounted a dais in the middle of the Market Place, accompanied by their Breton counterparts and sundry attendants. First in English, then in French, our mayor emphasised that the occasion was not simply a spree but rather a solemn undertaking whereby the two towns would henceforth encourage their young people to exchange visits, to share cultural activities, and to acquaint themselves with the quirks and customs of their twin across the water; in short, to become more European without growing either less French or less English. Did not Shakespeare himself look forward to the time when

> . . . English may as French, French Englishmen,
> Receive each other . . .

While Devon listened with uncomprehending approval, the French mayor—who spoke no English—blended courtesy and cordiality: "Messieurs, mesdames, mes amis . . ." He, too, hoped that the twins would profit from their mutual understanding. Then the charter was signed—one copy for each town—and the documents were held aloft while the crowd applauded, and the lady of Boolong cried: "Veevee la Fronze!"

Slowly the townsfolk dispersed; swiftly the taverns overflowed; gaily the little groups fraternised, speaking an Esperanto of nods and smiles and handshakes. Those of us who had endured two world wars and a lifetime of "liberation movements" were not likely to indulge rosy daydreams; yet when we glanced again at the youth of two nations, arm-linked in amity, the sight of their unison recalled Miranda's faith:

> How many goodly creatures are there here!
> How beauteous mankind is! O, brave new world,
> That has such people in't!

The Cool of the Evening

Since early morning the sun had shone so fiercely that even its worshippers were satiated. At noon the dahlias began to wilt. At teatime—with the thermometer in the eighties—all activity ceased. Not a leaf stirred, not a bird sang. Harvesters huddled in the shadow of a combine; the stream scarcely trickled; the air hung like an invisible blanket; and cats coiled themselves in the darkest corner of a barn while cows stood beside the parched ford, wondering where the water had gone. When the harvesters resumed work they knotted their handkerchiefs to make a sun helmet. Holidaymakers on the cliff exchanged curt greetings: "Bit much, eh?"

At six o'clock a cottager emerged from his porch, blinked at the glare, and then started to weed the flower beds, but only those of them that were shaded by the wall. Calling at The Three Anvils for an aperitif, a homeward harvester confessed: "I'm that thirsty I could swallow a flipping brewery." This was the hour, and such the mood, when dusty travellers ignored their destination, gladly accepting the hospitality that was offered on the road to Emmaus: "Abide with us: for it is toward evening, and the day is far spent."

At eight o'clock, with the sun sinking steeply, the air grew cool enough to invite a stroll despite the midges that still forced the farmer to light a pipe of fumigating tobacco. Shadows climbed midway up the highbanked lane, enhancing some pink foxgloves in sunlight on the upper half. The boles of beeches astride the bank were steeped in gold. Silent since noon, a thrush sang, not with the abandon of dawn, but serenely like a poet who has mastered the art to which he gave his life.

Suddenly a wisp of cloud dimmed the sun, rinsing the sky paler than light blue and lighter than pale grey. Against that slight haze the wild roses and cow-parsley stood out like white discs beside a lane draped with red berries, lilac teasels, purple vetches. Presently came a brown butterfly, dappled with orange spots; and above the butterfly came a kestrel, justifying its name as "wind-hover". Swifter than a falling stone, the bird swooped to treetop level, feeding on crane-flies. Then, for no apparent reason, it sheered away toward the moor. Sharper than men, the kestrel had sighted a sparrow-hawk skimming the hedgerows. Refracted by haze, the sun seemed to set the sky on fire, scorching the tufts of lady's bedstraw, which old people called "cheese rennet" because their grandparents had used it as a milk curdler. The rose-bay willow herb mimed an attenuated lupin alongside yellow toadflax that resembled an antirrhinum. Deciduous trees had long ago merged their Maytime freshness in a uniform dark green, but the lime could be identified via its ripening fruits. When at last the sun sank behind a hill, the warmth went with it.

Now a late bee hurries home, anxious as a man who has lingered too long at the tavern. The insect's course really is a bee-line. In fact, you duck to avoid being hit. Perched on a gatepost, the thrush concludes his Evensong with a tranquil Amen, unlike the rooks' raucous lullaby. After twelve sweltering hours you are surprised to feel a slight shiver creeping up your bare forearm, sent there by what Robert Nicols called

> the surf
> Of the midsummer wind among the boughs . . .

The lane grows dusky now, and the moon peers above the trees, as it were counting the stars that play hide-and-seek between the branches. A wild rose gleams whiter than ever, but the yellow toadflax has faded, and the lady's bedstraw blends with the other grasses, all pallid in astringent twilight. Unrolling your shirtsleeves, you quicken the pace, part-glad yet part-sad that the heat and burden of the day have abated.

On the way home you hear a faint barking from the opposite hill. Was it a dog? A fox? The next bark is loud enough to betray the long-eared owl, a beige-coloured creature, speckled with grey and brown. Challenged by the owl, three larks leap up, too dim to be seen, though shrill enough to ripple the stillness with a music which caused John Clare to belittle his own,

> Making amid their strains divine
> All songs in vain so mean as mine.

While the western sky snuffs the last ember of its final spark, the moon shines unchallenged, imprinting all things with the black-and-whiteness of a negative photograph. When you step on them, the shadows of trees perform a sleight-of-sight by treading on your toes. A murmur proves that the stream still trickles. A cough announces that the cows still stand beside the ford, fly-free at last, each animal so blanched by the moon that Jerseys and Friesians can no longer be recognised from their colour. Although the grass remains warm, the breeze strikes chilly. You glance at your watch. In another six hours the blue sky will introduce another warm day.

These last moments of August are a prolonged farewell to summer. Their mood is elegiac, touched by remembrance of mortality. You look up, as if the leaves and already turned brown; then you look down, as if the breeze had already veered north. For the first time since April you think of frost and firelight. A thousand centuries echo the plaint of innumerable voices: "I dread the winter." If, however, the summer has fulfilled most of its promises, then the cool evening seems less a lament than a benediction, for you have had your share of warmth, and are ready to receive the autumn's crisper climate.

9

George and the Dragons

Members of the farming fraternity are easily identified on market days, when they stand in small groups outside the guildhall, rather like conspirators who have come either to praise Caesar or to bury him, the choice being settled by the price of beef and the state of the weather. Older members of the fraternity dress very much as their fathers did, and some of their accoutrements may actually have been purchased during the Siege of Mafeking . . . things such as belts and walking sticks and pocket watches.

On market day in deep country many of the yeoman farmers wear a raincoat. If the temperature exceeds seventy degrees Fahrenheit the coat may be slung over a shoulder. Generally, however, it is worn as a talisman against the elements. Tweed caps are the favourite headgear, with gumboots sometimes replacing the more formal brown boots, which are highly polished and reminiscent of small cottage loaves. Leggings or gaiters remain *de rigueur* in rough weather. Most farmers carry a walking stick, either to lean on or to prod with. On the way to market they quiz their neighbours' land as keenly as did Robert Frost's countryman:

> You ought to have seen what I saw on my way
> To the village, through Paterson's pasture today . . .

The old nickname for farmers was George, from the Greek *georgos* or husbandman (one, that is, who nurtures and tills the soil). King George III became so interested in farming that he was known affectionately as "Farmer George". It is difficult to

decide whether the resemblances between a farmer in 1977 and a
farmer in 1777 are more remarkable than the differences. Thus, a
farmer still spends most of his working life in the open air. He
still rises early, still blames the weather, still curses the government, still clings to precedent, and—like a physician—still
combines science with intuition. Technology has not yet devised
a computer that will tell the farmer when to reap and whether to
plough.

Farmers still carry a gun now and again, if only to scare the
pigeons. Many of them approve hunting, and some indulge it,
like the Victorian squire who told Richard Jefferies: "Whether
it is hunting, or shooting, or coursing, or racing, there is something in it which lifts one out of the vapidness of life . . . where
one hunted years ago, ten hunt now; where one gun was sold
then, twenty are sold now." Toward gardening, however, the
farmer feels less enthusiastic: "I leave that sort of thing to the
wife". His concern with herbs has been outmoded by pharma-
cology, and his knowledge of wild flowers has been poisoned by
insecticides; yet he retains an eye for such things, and will sometimes use the old names . . . peagle, kurlick, snapdragon. As in
1777 so in 1977, a farmer knows what it is to hack the ice from a
starlit cattle trough on Christmas morning; to sweat in a hayfield
on Midsummer Eve; to rescue snowbound ewes, and deliver
stillborn lambs, and call the cows home at sundown. He must
recognise the symptoms of colic and fluke and pregnancy. He
must hammer a stake when he would rather drink a pint. He must
repair a gate, answer a letter, clear a drain, and grease an axle.
Without changing his basic routine, technology has gone a long
way toward turning the farmer inside-out and upside-down. For
example, lambing time is nowadays any time between mid-
winter and late spring. Fruits and flowers that were formerly
obtainable only during a brief season are on sale for months
at a stretch. Some skills, like scything and handmilking, have
almost disappeared; others, like cheese-making and bee-keeping,
no longer rank among the duties of a farmstead.

In the years when Britain could feed herself without needing
either to beg or to borrow, the tenant farmers were by no means
adept at reading and writing. Their day's work done, they sat
by the fire or relaxed in the shade. Even when literacy became
common, Farmer George seldom perused anything beyond his

local newspaper and a technical magazine. William Cobbett was reared on a farm that lacked even a headline: "I do not remember," he wrote, "ever having seen a newspaper in the house, and most certainly the privation did not render us less free, or happy, or industrious." Then came progress in the guise of ministries, questionnaires, and planning permission to mend a gap in the hedge. George, in fact, was surrounded by dragons who dragooned him into acting as his own secretary-cum-computer; and if anyone now dares to criticise any aspect of that bureaucracy, he is labelled as a Luddite, an advocate of handlooms and garden privies.

A farmer may be a gentleman, but the gentleman-farmer has vanished insofar as his grandmother would scarcely recognise him as such. Instead of hunting three days a week, and shooting and fishing whenever the law allows, many of the heirs of the landed gentry now type their own invoices, and help to shear their own sheep. Few can afford to leave everything to an agent or bailiff.

Ruskin challenged a Victorian fallacy when he attacked the so-called "science of political economy, based on the idea that an advantageous code of social action may be determined irrespectively of the influence of social affection." For more than a century the British have exploited the farmer's "social affection," trusting that it will bind him to the land even when the land has been sacrificed to industry. Cobbett and Jefferies both described the plight of farmers who, late in life, were forced to sell their furniture and to seek work as labourers, utterly ruined by rising wages, falling prices, and the nation's obsession with exported hardware. Cobbett himself, son of a Surrey peasant-farmer, explained why it is that some men till the soil as much for love as for money: "Born amongst husbandmen, bred to husbandry, delighting in its pursuits, never having, in all my range of life, lost sight of the English farmhouse and of those scenes in which my mind took its first spring, it is natural that I should have a strong partiality for country life . . ."

The Last Rites of Summer

The landowner who says he is too busy to trim his hedges is like the helmsman who says he is too busy to steer his ship. If hedges are allowed to run amok they fail to provide an adequate windbreak for livestock and crops. Hedges ought to be leafy and close-knit to a height of four or five feet; above that level they rob the adjacent soil of sunlight and ventilation.

Many of the lanes in these parts are only just wide enough to take a car, and by the end of June the overhanging branches and briars need to be cut back. If this is not done, vehicles get scratched while cyclists get wounded. One of my own fields overlooks just such a lane, and in midsummer it is trimmed by a farmhand. During September it is re-trimmed by myself. The task occupies less than an hour, and is time well spent, as anyone knows, who, at ten o'clock in the morning, has watched the sun disperse an autumnal mist, unveiling a blue sky. Choosing an auspicious day, therefore, I proceed to tidy-up, armed with leather gauntlets and a sharp blade.

The lane itself is steep as well as narrow. In fact, the field overlooks the stiffest contour of a one-in-three gradient. The far side of the lane dips to a combe and then climbs to a lofty ridge of woodland and pasture. To say that nobody ever uses the lane is a colloquial way of stating that in autumn the traffic averages two vehicles a day . . . the milkwoman in a van and the farmer on a tractor. During August I once counted as many as three vehicles in six hours, but such traffic jams are neither seen nor heard from the house.

There is something modestly complacent in the performance of a duty whose results are private. Nobody, I believe, has ever seen me trimming the embankment. Strangers might not notice that I had done so, were it not for the unkempt hedges on the other tracts of the lane, parts of which have been neglected for years, and are nearly as high as a house. So, under a hot sun and to the tune of humming insects, the grass and briars are slashed away, leaving a green-and-brown tidemark in the lane. A certain amount of amateur botanising takes place during the work. One identifies the common plants—bracken, blackberries, nettles, docks—

together with the relics of dog's mercury, herb robin, snowdrops, anemones, celandines, violets, primroses, bluebells, foxgloves. In short, the lane is a kind of calendar, recording the birth of spring and the burial of winter.

How easy it is to recognise, yet how difficult to define, the look of the land in September. A quick glance may deny that autumn has arrived, for the shaded beech and the riverside meadow still glow as green as in July. Garden flowers still span the spectrum, and the white clouds dapple a blue sky. Closer examination, however, tells the truth. Oak leaves and bracken bear the brown marks of age. The grass, too, is brown, especially during a dry spell. Every shadow is a sundial, showing Earth's progress round the sun. And where are the birds of yesterspring, those tireless food-ferries? They are in the shade, silent after an August moulting and the last late brood. Only the robin has much to say, cocky as a member of the choir was suddenly finds himself singing solo. Next month his voice will sound above the sigh of falling leaves and the moan of rising wind.

"Golden" is a favourite September adjective among the poets. A blue-and-white sky really does seem to be tinctured by the stubble; so also do the shafts of sunlight slanting through the trees. The dust itself seems golden; and if the landscape shows a field of standing corn, then the yellow radiance really does catch the eye, distracting it from all other colours. But the gilt is very thin on a season whose sunsets may unfold Mary Webb's setpiece,

> When autumn winds are on the hill
> And darkly rides the wasting moon . . .

After half-an-hour the trimming invites a rest, so I lean against the bank, sampling the sunny silence. Far away on the opposite hill a farmhouse glistens white. In the middle distance a red stag strolls leisurely into a coppice. Midges tread the mill of a sunbeam that falls like an intangible pillar across the lane. Three feet above my head, a robin sits on a spray of bracken, quizzing the debris. When I collect that debris, and set fire to it, the robin flies to a safer perch on the holly tree. Now the pungent smoke climbs like an Indian rope until, breasting the bank, it meets a breeze, and is zigzagged away. Everything is so dry that a single spark may catch fire. However, the hedge has been shorn, and no passer-by will complain that a briar has grazed his cheek. Standing guard over the bonfire, I lose count of time, but when I look up at the sun, I see that I have spent more than a dozen minutes alternately feeding and compressing the fire. When at last the smoke subsides, the ashes are grey dust in the middle of the lane, as it were a pyre, from which the autumn and the winter will evoke another spring.

Some people regard hedge-trimming as a trivial chore, on a par with brushing one's teeth; necessary, no doubt, but scarcely a topic of conversation. The world, they say, would soon be in a sorry state if we spent our time wandering up and down the country lanes of Britain. True; yet the world would soon be in a less sorry state if we were able to rusticate some of those people who spend their time wandering up and down the corridors of power. When set in its proper place, trimming a hedge gives an active answer to a famous question:

> What is this life, if, full of care,
> We have no time to stand and stare?

Moving with the Times

Halfway up the hill I overtook my old friend, the Chiltern cottager. "Oi thought oi 'eard footsteps," he said. Then he glanced at the sky. "Just roight for an evening stroll."

We were both surprised to see each other, because I seldom visit those parts, though at one time they were my home. While we climbed the lane, I recalled our first meeting long ago, when I had noticed that all the man's movements were ponderous. At our second meeting, however, I decided that "ponderous" was not the appropriate adjective, so I substituted "slow". An hour later I discovered that "slow" begged the question, for did not a tortoise once outpace its swifter rival? Several other epithets were tried—"measured" and "leisurely" and "relaxed"—until at last I chose the word "natural". Now the busybodies who specialise in time and motion study will protest that "natural" begs another question. Confronted by an angry bull, they will say, it is not at all "natural" for anyone to remain leisurely and relaxed. On the contrary, a reflex secretion of adrenalin quickens our responses, often enabling portly persons to avoid the fate of the matador who did *not* get away. Nevertheless, I maintain that "natural" is the nearest description of the movements of certain countrymen, and I base my claim on the fact that those country-men move in rhythm with Nature itself. This is especially notice-able in the unhurried actions of a hedger or a scyther. Indeed, an absence of unnecessary haste is part of such men's attitude to life.

The old bachelor, meanwhile, must have been reading my thoughts, because, when we paused for breath on the summit, he exclaimed: "The race is neither to the swift nor to the slow." Then, as though aware that his version was unauthorised, he added: "The charp wart wins is 'im as gits there first. But the trouble nowadays is, everyone warnts to git there first. Even when they go abroad they tell you 'ow long it took 'em. Step insoide and oi'll put a march to it."

The last sentence was an invitation to enter his cottage while he lit a fire. Once again, therefore, I observed the unhurried skill with which he chopped part of a crate into kindling wood; the suppleness with which he stooped over the hearth, slightly bending at the knees; and the stately clop of his axe in the porch. Standing on the threshold, with an armful of logs, he cocked his head to listen to a blackbird. "Thart old blackie don't pull no wool over my eyes. In September it gits a bit nippy arter sundown."

He set a match to the wood. "Man is born to trouble as the sparks fly upwards," he mused. "But if there warn't so sparks oi don't reckon as we'd manage to git born at all. We'd just freeze to death." As the logs began to crackle he resumed the topic of movement. "Take young Gurney," he suggested. "Ten o'clock last noight, when oi was leaving The Wheatsheaf, oi 'ears Gurney revving 'is car down the lane. Three jiffies later 'ee's 'ome again, so oi says to 'im, 'Where you bin?' and 'ee says, 'To post a letter.' But the pillarbox warn't above foive minutes walk. 'And anyow,' oi says, 'the post don't go till Monday.' "

"What did he say to that?"

"His exact words were, 'You're living in the bloody Dark Ages.' " The old man relaxed in his rocking chair. "Only last week," he recalled, "the vicar were telling me the words of the poet."

"Oh? Which poet?"

"Fella called Andrew Marvellous. Always in an 'urry were Andrew. 'Whenever oi droive a chariot,' he wrote, 'oi can 'ear the wings o'Toime grazing my barksoide.' Ah, and 'ee warn't the only one. Take the new ploughman, for instance. Eight o'clock Ted's supposed to start. Well, at ten-past oi 'ears 'is car racing downhill. At midday it races up again, then races down, and then sixty-moile-an-hour 'ome at telytoime. It don't make sense." He tapped a log with his toecap. "Everyone's in a tizzy nowadays," he complained. "But it warn't always so. When oi ploughed a field oi took it steady, and at the end o' the day oi'd done a better job nor them as wore 'emselves out afore dinner. And oi'll tell you summat else. The faster you do go the faster you've got to keep going. Oi don't care wart it is . . . playing darts or making a motor car . . . once you gits in a tizzy your loife ain't worth living. Take this 'ere Discord . . ."

"Discord?"

"Thart's wart oi calls it. The new airyplane across the Atlantic. The one as breaks the sound barrier and then smashes your eardrums. Millions and millions it costs, all so's a bunch o' fat paunches can arroive a bit earlier." He spat politely into the fire. "It'd do 'em a soight more good if they was to swim there. And if some of 'em sank you wouldn't git me shedding no tears." Suddenly he leaned forward, keen as an inquisitor. "You ever hoed a field?"

"I have."

"Ever troid to rush it?"

"Occasionally."

"And wart 'appened?"

"I had to start all over again."

"There you are, see? It's loike wart the Prayer Book says. Have patience, it says, 'cause them as renews their strength shall fly faster than heagles." He resumed an even keel. "But oi keeps my mouth shut nowadays. 'T'aint no use trying to tell 'em. If they warn't the chariot to graze their barksoides, thart's their own affair. As for meself, oi've never got toime to be in an 'urry."

In a Country Churchyard

Recalling his friendship with Thomas Hardy, John Masefield once said to me: "Tom was never so happy as when brooding in a graveyard." That obsession with decay reminds one of the schoolboy who translated *memento mori* as 'Remember to die'. At the other end of the scale are the people who, in their eagerness to sound witty, either forget or do not care that a joke about death may pierce the mourner's heart, even although the bereavement occurred decades ago.

The epitaphs in a country churchyard reveal that our articulate response to grief may be changed by the spirit of the age. From time to time someone publishes a selection of those epitaphs, but their impact is seldom so moving as that of the inscriptions which we have discovered for ourselves. Certain temperaments feel that the most poignant elegies are not expressed in words, but appear as brasses showing a husband and wife and their five small children; victims, perhaps, of an infection which could nowadays be cured by a chemist. Medieval folk were concerned rather to confess their sins than to subscribe their merits. They rarely composed the orotund paeans so dear to the eighteenth century. The earliest record of a rhymed epitaph comes from Holme-next-the-Sea in Norfolk, and is six centuries old. It does praise the deceased, but solely for their parochial benefactions:

> Henry Notyngham and hys wyffe lyne here,
> Yat made this chirche stepull and quere,
> Two vestments and belles they made also,
> Christ save them therefore from wo.

Even more modest is the epitaph of a man whose birth and achievements might have caused him to be eulogised *ad nauseam*. The man was George Herbert, the Caroline poet and a kinsman to the Earl of Pembroke, who forwent a brilliant career at Court in order to become vicar of an obscure Wiltshire parish. A plaque on the chancel wall at Fugglestone Saint Peter bears nothing more than his initials: "G.H."

Then came the fondness for circumlocutional eloquence, as at Sibton in Suffolk, where a memorial states that Marianne

I

Scrivener was destined "To be placed among the angels for whose society she so early qualified." Another East Anglian worthy, Sheriff John Reynolds of Felsham, seems to have spent his days in a minority of one, for the tomb declares that "he thought differently from all other men while he lived." In 1733, at Shelsley Walsh in Shropshire, they buried Elizabeth Plampin, whose husband mourned her as

> Devout without Superstition
> Reverent without Indecency.

Sometimes an epitaph is the work of a true poet, like the lines that were composed by Robert Herrick, vicar of Dean Prior in Devon, for his faithful housekeeper:

> In this little Urne is laid
> Prewdence Baldwin (once my maid)
> From whose happy spark here let
> Spring the purple violet.

At Lancercost in Cumberland an epitaph to a member of the great Howard family confirms that death is no respecter of persons:

> Twenty years a maiden,
> One year a wife,
> One hour a mother,
> Then departed life.

Not every memorial recalls a human being. At Stoke Pero in Somerset a tablet on the church wall says: "Be Thou praised my Lord with all thy Creatures. In the year 1897, when this church was restored, Zulu, a donkey, walked twice a day from Parson Street, Porlock, bearing all the oak used in the roof." Since Stoke Pero church is the highest on Exmoor, more than a thousand feet above Porlock, one wonders why no tablet has recorded the stamina of the men who led Zulu up and down the one-in-three lane through Horner Woods. Not every memorial is in a church or a churchyard. Near the saw-mill at Dilston in Northumberland a gravestone pays tribute to a faithful dog:

> In Memoriam. Portos O.B.
> August 14, 1899. Fidus ad Extremum.

The unacceptable face of nationalism is carved on a plinth in a field near the church at Kirharle (Northumbrian birthplace of

'Capability' Brown), stating that the squire, Robert Loraine, "was barbarously murdered in this place by the Scots in 1483, for his good services to his country against their thefts and robberies, as he was returning from the church alone, where he had been at his private devotions."

In the Breconshire village of Vaynor an isolated church overlooks the rocky banks of the lesser Taf River. It was built by Robert Crashaw, a Victorian industrialist, on the site of an earlier church; and there they buried Crashaw himself, with his own three-word memorial: "God forgive me." John Wesley wrote an epitaph for an old Cornishwoman who was still alive: "Her sons are all gone from her; and she has but one daughter left, who is always ill. Her husband is dead; and she can no longer read her Bible, for she is stone-blind. Yet she murmurs nothing, but cheerfully waits till her appointed time shall come. How many of these jewels may lie hid; forgotten of men, but precious in the sight of God!"

Briefer, though no less memorable, is a couplet by the Tudor poet, James Shirley, which sweeps away all the pretension of the famous and all the hypocrisy of the obscure:

> Only the actions of the just
> Smell sweet, and blossom in their dust.

10

Fairyland

What a beautiful county Shropshire is, the shire with Shrewsbury as capital. The Saxons called it *Scrobbesbyrigscir*, a sound so sibilant that the Normans renamed it *Salopescire*, whence 'Salop' and 'Salopian'. Shrewsbury long ago dwarfed its historic buildings with a commercial skyline, but the fame of the place abides, broadcast by David Garrick, who, while still a schoolboy, made his first theatrical appearance when actor-managing *The Recruiting Officer*, which Farquhar dedicated in the words of an old Salopian toast "To all round the Wrekin." Shrewsbury School nurtured *inter alios* Sir Philip Sidney, Charles Darwin, and a number of rowing Blues.

Mary Webb called Shrewsbury "My own town." A few miles beyond it, on the slopes of Lyth Hill, stands the house which she and her husband built, in a smallholding whose produce they sold at Shrewsbury market. As a writer, Mary Webb died almost unknown. Shortly after her death, however, a much-publicised speech praising her poetry and prose was delivered by the prime minister, Stanley Baldwin; and on the following day the unknown author became famous. Her neglected novel, *Precious Bane*, was reprinted a dozen times in a dozen months. Her poems and essays were reprinted twenty times in twenty years. Mary Webb may have foreseen the reward which she did not live to enjoy, because, in a poem about Shrewsbury, she predicted:

> And I shall live where once unknown
> I passed, and all shall be my own,
> For I have built of joy and tears
> A city that defies the years.

As with Emily Brontë and Yorkshire, so with Mary Webb and Shropshire; neither of the women could endure to live away from her native county, and each won fame by portraying it. "Places where the fairies might dwell," said G. M. Trevelyan, "lie for the most part west of the Avon." In so saying he set the scene for the secret places of Mary Webb's Shropshire, where, as she claimed, "the dignity and beauty of ancient things lingers long . . . a magical atmosphere."

Walking through the heart of that magic, not far from Church Stretton, I left the loud main road, following a narrow lane which led into the hills, not as a continuous ascent but as a rhythmic switchback. On the third summit—or it may have been the fourth —I halted. Westward the mountains stood like sleepless sentries over Cymru; eastward the sandstone Saxon acres unfolded a green carpet flecked with pink. Everywhere the pastures shone, refreshed by recent rain. Woods and coverts gleamed like copper, and the fallen leaves wove a circle at the foot of beeches. Presently a blackbird landed on a sycamore, repeating verbatim the sentiments of his sires a thousand years ago. When the song ended, the stillness seemed more assertive than sound, as though to justify the poet's declamation:

> I love the Welshbound March,
> The frontier, the deep
> Combe and the forest larch
> Where still the fairies sleep
> (Or so men say) that wake
> When magic daysprings break.

Twelve centuries ago, when King Offa built his Dyke, this part of Shropshire was a No Man's Land dividing fierce enemies; but now the pastures painted a peaceful picture of sunlight buffing the burnished leaves, of raindrops rinsing the russet bracken, of curlews culling the new-turned furrow. Here indeed the edge of England touched the rim of Wales. Had Dafydd ap Gwilym been a Saxon, he might have chosen this spot as his home: "My *haford* and my *hendre*."

After a few miles I entered a village, but was careful to forget the name lest news of it spread. The next lap brought me to the foot of yet another hill. Glancing up, I noticed a curious object coming over the brow. Then the object revealed itself as a battered hat above a weathered face beneath a white beard astride a Welsh cob. As the rider came alongside he confirmed that in Shropshire "the dignity and beauty of ancient things lingers long."

"Sir," he said, slowly dismounting, "I have lost three sheep. Cluns. They are close to my heart and dear to my pocket. Have you seen them?"

"In that meadow down there," I replied, pointing over my shoulder, "I did notice some sheep."

The veteran tethered his cob, and we went to look. Sure enough, the sheep were there.

"Three," murmured Methuselah. "Cluns. Mine. I am greatly obliged to you." He raised his hat, holding it high for several moments while a breeze rippled the mane of white hair. Then he strode away, an old man into autumn, yet nimble as Narcissus in the spring.

Having reached the summit, I glanced to my left, and saw the farmer leading three ewes, followed by a collie. Halfway up the next hill he overtook me on his cob.

"Even in heaven," he remarked, "they are glad to recover their strays." He rose in the stirrups, like a sailor sighting a landfall. "This," he said, "is a beautiful land."

"Very," I agreed.

"Yet they tell me there are lands even more beautiful."

"Mere travellers' tales," I assured him.

"That may be so." He quizzed the sun. "Half-past noon," he reckoned, "and no rest for the man with three wicked ewes." Once more the hat was raised. "I wish you good-day."

"Your wish," I replied, "has come true."

The Salopian gave a slight nod, rather as though I were a pupil who had supplied the correct answer. Then he clucked, and the cob carried him over the brow and down into Eden.

Gale Warning

This is no ordinary gale. It is an aftermath of the autumnal equinox, a truly thunderous cavalcade of Valkyrie riding in from the north-west, flailing whatever they cannot flatten. Six fallen elms block the lane to the sea, and one of them has crashed onto a cottage whose occupant stands in her garden, staring at the roofless upper storey. She cannot telephone for help, because the wires, too, have been swept away.

The movements of a tree usually vary with the force of the wind, but today every bough maintains a constant quivering, as though the wind were so violent that only a slight shudder is possible, each bough being pressed back before it can bend too far forward. Grass in the meadow seems not to move at all, but is flattened uniformly until an especially brutal gust compels the blades to right themselves and then collapse again, like victims pleading with their torturer. Yesterday the lane was strewn with dead leaves; now it appears to have been swept by a broom that has tossed the leaves over the hedge, or into a close-packed mound underneath it, their place being taken by fallen twigs and branches.

Sailors still classify wind velocity according to a scale that was devised in 1805 by Captain (afterwards Admiral) Sir Francis

Beaumont, who listed twelve forces of wind, ranging from calm
to hurricane. These include four types of gale—moderate, fresh,
strong, whole—whose velocities rise from thirty-two to sixty-
three nautical miles an hour. After them come storm and hurricane
with wind speeds rising from sixty-four to more than seventy-six
nautical miles an hour, and waves more than forty-five feet high
and nearly two thousand feet long. Beaufort, of course, lived in
the days of sail. He therefore described a strong breeze (force six)
as "that which a well-conditioned ship of war could just carry in
chase, 'full and by', single-reefed topsails and topgallant sails,
and fishing smacks double-reef gaff mainsails." Today's gale is
force ten, as wild as any that ever strikes Britain.

Meantime, the streets of the little harbour are deserted, and
you judge the power of the wind by observing the extent to
which it has carried the spume inland. One cobbled alley, more
than two hundred yards from the waterfront, shines with spray,
and a window of the Customs House is plastered with seaweed.
Every few seconds a wave strikes the jetty with a thud which
your feet can feel, even although your ears fail to hear it above
the general din. Like a gigantic Indian rope trick, each crest
uncoils its own white ladder, and hovers briefly on the topmost
rung, seeming to claw the air. Then it collapses onto the cobbles,
and this time you do hear it, an indescribable sound, somewhere
between the crack of a whip and the hiss of molten fat.

Presently you notice a small group of people in the lee of a
quayside shelter. Five of them are women, each wearing a shawl
over their heads. The youngest woman—hardly more than a girl
—holds a child's hand. Fishing and sailing being out of the
question, you are puzzled to account for the group; but when the
girl raises the child in her arms, you solve the puzzle intuitively
. . . they have launched the lifeboat, and there she goes, creeping
seaward, sheltered by the jetty. A minute later she loses the
shelter, rearing up until it seems that she must topple backwards.
Even if you are a sailor you will find it difficult to believe that
such a tiny craft could survive in such a mountainous sea. If you
are a landsman you may refuse to believe it, and will therefore
turn away, partly because the mere sight of the switchback makes
you feel dizzy, and partly because you are convinced that the boat
will be swamped by the next wave, or fail to rise from the next
gulf. After what seems an eternity the little craft is still visible,

rhythmic as a cork on a windswept pond. Keen eyes can detect the threshing screws whenever she poises herself for the downward rush; but no eye at all can find her when she wallows in a trough. Eventually the little group disperses, hurrying home with heads bent against the storm. But someone—you cannot tell whether it is a man or a woman—someone remains on the jetty, staring, hoping, fearing.

On your way back, passing the Customs House, you see the cars and motor-cycles of the men who have offered their lives, not knowing whether the gift will be returned to them. Capsized by the wind, one of the motor-cycles has slipped within range of the spray, and lies there like a helpless ship. Seeing it, a member of the returning group retrieves the ill omen. Through a gap in the hedge near the roofless cottage you glance down at the jetty and the curdling waves. Whence came the cry for help? From the listing bridge of a tanker far out to sea? From the waterlogged engine room of a coaster in sight of

> Death's very self, wide-opening his door,
> The anchors useless, and the breakers close . . .?

Whether near or far, the lifeboat will obey her sailing orders:

> Gladly our seamen answered as they neared;
> In that blind peril brave heart answered heart . . .

The sea, you fancy, strives to drown that cry for help; but the crew of the lifeboat have heard, and are responding with an everlasting Yea.

Men who go down to the sea in ships may find therein a famous grave, alongside Drake and Grenville. But courage and seamanship outnumber the scrolls of fame. The men of the lifeboat service are content to share Masefield's collective anonymity:

> O memory, praise them, before Death efface.

A Modern Scholar Gipsy

Once a year, at the start of the Michaelmas Term, Mr Chips, the retired schoolmaster, dines *de jure* as Fellow Commoner at high table in his old college. This festively erudite occasion concludes a week of rural roaming among the scenes of his Oxford youth, during which he lodges with a widow whose cottage has been receiving him for nearly half a century. Indeed, he spent some of his first long vacation there, as one of a reading party.

The cottage itself stands on the edge of a village familiar to Matthew Arnold's scholar gipsy. In that land of hills and streams Mr Chips not only revives old memories but also creates new ones; sometimes walking, sometimes boating, sometimes cycling; always knickerbockered, tweed-jacketed, black-shoed, and wearing a deer-stalker hat. When revisiting the site of the college barges he sports the Leander tie which he earned by rowing bow in the eight that went head of the river. More often than not, October smiles on his annual pilgrimage, so that he may be seen

> Crossing the stripling Thames at Bab-lock-hithe,

or, from the twilit Cumnor Hills, turning to watch

> The line of festal lights in Christ-Church hall . . .

Once, when the weather was especially mild, he camped for the night

> On the skirts of Bagley wood,
> Where most the Gipsies by the turf-edged way
> Pitch their smoked tents . . .

Since Mr Chips knew Oxford before it was taken over by Mammon, he flinches from the proliferation of factories and houses, for he can never feel certain that on his next visit a favourite meadow, or a well-loved lane, will not have been buried beneath concrete. Even in the Oxfordshire Chilterns he must pick and choose a route; even at Maidensgrove, even at Christmas Common, even at Russells Water. Only once has he failed to keep pace with progress, and that was when he noticed two unkempt characters prowling round the main quadrangle after dark, one of them barefooted, no doubt to avoid detection. Having been a special constable, Mr Chips (DSO, RA), kept the suspects under observation, and was not at all surprised when the shoeless vagabond removed a bunch of bananas from an open window, whispering to his accomplice: "Findings keepings, says Chairman Mao." In recounting the episode to the Sub-Dean, Mr Chips remarked: "I immediately summoned the porter. But he, poor fellow, merely held up his hands and said, 'I regret to inform you, Sir, that those two persons are members of this college.' " Mr Chips then closed the matter with a sigh: "*Tempora mutantur*. All the same, I do wish that some of the youths had signed on at a university whose ethos is more in keeping with their passion for bare feet and mob rule."

Dinner at high table remains much the same as when Mr Chips first surveyed it from the Freshmen's Gallery half a century ago. Portraits of poets and bishops and statesmen still from their panelled niche peer down on gleaming silver and pink-shaded table lamps. The old heads are still bald, and although the young ones have grown shaggy, the carefree laughter and the Latin toasts retain their orotund echo *in saecula saeculorum*.

After dinner, in the Senior Common Room, Mr Chips begins to feel that time has not after all marched on; but then the Vice-Provost refutes him with an *ipse dixit*: "Gibbon was the last man of whom it can be said that he knew everything that was known about the Roman Empire. Nowadays we're required to confine ourselves to a single emperor. They tell me it's much the same with biology . . . not that I was ever greatly interested in tadpoles and that sort of thing. The point is, a man's field of study has become so narrow that it will soon be little more than a garden lawn."

At eleven o'clock, when the others have departed, Mr Chips draws his chair closer to the octogenarian who tutored him to a First in Greats. Together, over a third glass of port, they discuss his own long-awaited paper on Housman and Manilius. An hour later—the ritual never varies—the two scholars go their ways, each wondering whether they will meet again next year.

In the porter's lodge Mr Chips unlocks his Sunbeam bicycle (renovated 1925), steers it onto the pavement, and stands there listening until in deep tones Great Tom repeats the chimes that were heard at midnight long ago, and is answered by the bells of the city as they announce the birth of a new day; some treble, some bass, all prevailing above the screech of a car and the rumble of a lorry. When the last carillon has died away, Mr Chips slowly wheels his machine down the High, often pausing to glance up at the towered and turreted silhouettes while he murmurs a couplet from Quiller-Couch:

> Still on the spire the pigeons flutter,
> Still by the gateway flits the gown . . .

Half an hour later, at the brow of a hill, he dismounts and once again listens. Sure enough, faint on a frosty air, the distant chimes reach him, the soul of Oxford speaking above the bric-à-brac of commerce. After a few more miles he reaches the widow's cottage, where an oil lamp shines from the porch. Soon he will enter, and creak upstairs to a raftered bedroom. For the moment, however, he leans on the handlebars, hearing the silence, tasting the air, seeing the stars; conscious that the twentieth century had righted many wrongs, yet thankful that he can remember the Oxfordshire countryside as it was

> Before this strange disease of modern life
> With its sick hurry, its divided aims . . .

Invitation to a Stag Party

All six of the watchers were keen-eyed, and each was looking for the same object, yet only one of them—a shepherd—saw the stag. This was not surprising, because the animal's colouring blended with a background of russet bracken and autumnal trees. Then, by moving, the stag betrayed himself to the five townsmen. "There he is!" they exclaimed.

Perhaps by chance, or perhaps because he had got wind of them, the stag glanced up, but instead of moving away he raised his head, pawed the ground, and uttered a hoarse roar. Being strangers to the game, the townsmen asked their guide for an explanation of the stag's behaviour. In September, they were told, the stags grow restive. They indulge symbolic battles, and may risk minor clashes. But in October, the rutting season, the sparring becomes so hostile that the bachelor herds disperse, each stag roaming the moor in search of hinds. A stag's roar, the shepherd continued, may signify either a command to his hinds or a warning to his rivals.

"There he is again!"

This time the stag appeared on the skyline, just long enough for the shepherd to parse the antlers. "Brow," he counted, "trey . . . and there's a three-a-top by the look on't." He turned to his audience. "About eight years old, that one. Up in Scotland they'd call 'en a Royal, but t'isn't a name we use on Exmoor."

Before the visitors could focus their glasses, the stag had vanished. Then, from another quarter, came a rival roar.

"Will they fight?"

"That depends," the shepherd replied. "But I'll tell 'ee this much ... t'ain't often October passes without someone finds a dead stag on the moor. They charge each other, see, and the loser gets a brow point through his ribs. Not that they'd attack a human being, mind. Not unless they'm provoked."

"So you judged his age by his antlers?"

"More or less. But the light ain't all that good now. And anyway you can't really judge till a stag's two years old, and even then you may need to get close to 'en. But by the time he's four he'll show a bay and perhaps a trey as well."

"What's the greatest number of points on a stag?"

"The record, you mean? Nobody knows. My grandmother claimed she'd counted twenty-six, but 'twas just after closing time, and her never did support the Temperance League. I've seen one with seventeen points. They'm like fingerprints."

"Why?"

"Because no two of 'em are exactly alike. What's more, the left side don't tally with the right, leastways not on any stag I ever saw. Food and the climate must have something to do with it. If a young stag survives three cold and hungry years you can be pretty certain his antlers won't grow as they ought."

"How," someone asked, "do you recognise an old stag?"

"Same as you recognise an old man. He starts what we call 'going back.' His points wither, and the top ones turn blunt, and the females take to winking at the young bucks. It's the same the world over. God made us all, men as well as beasts, and 'tis too late now to ask 'en to change His recipe. But as I was saying, earlier today, you can read all about it in a book called *Stag-Hunting*, written by Sir John Fortescue."

"We saw his memorial, didn't we, on the road above Simonsbath?"

"That's the one. A great sportsman was Sir John. Ah, and a great writer, too. He was librarian at Windsor Castle, I believe, and he wrote a history of the British Army. The Fortescues are still the principal family in this part o' Devon. Been yere for centuries. But like a lot of the old families nowadays, they don't own as much land as they did. More's the pity, I say, 'cause they took care o' their property and o' their people."

The light was failing now, and the first stars appeared, twinkling on a green sky. The Exmoor heights glowed black as charcoal while bracken changed from bronze to darkest brown, and frost fingered its way through gloves.

"Time we packed it in," the shepherd decided. "Not even Lucifer could spot a stag in this light."

On the way home the shepherd told his party that October's mating would come to fruition when the calves were dropped in June, each calf being dappled, and twins uncommon. After about three months the calves would lose their spots; at four months they would begin to show the same red coat as the adults. "But you won't often see the mothers during daylight. They hide their calf in the undergrowth and then they steal away and keep watch from a distance. And they won't come back to feed 'en till near nightfall. Nowadays, of course, 'tis all protected by law."

It was dark when the party reached the inn. Logs blazed on a vast hearth, and the walls were lined with antlers and with pictures of past huntsmen and famous hounds.

"They've a regular museum in yere," the shepherd observed. "Stags get fresh horns every twelvemonth, usually round about April. The new growth is covered with a velvety skin so sensitive the stags avoid any tree that might strike their head. You could almost call it a moulting season. Anyway, it lasts till the end of summer, and by that time the horn gets so itchy the stags take to using the trees as a rubbing post."

"About hunting . . ." someone asked, but the shepherd stopped him. "No hunting," he warned, "and no politics neither. Once you'm on *those* subjects you may as well lose your temper and have done with it."

Terminus

The grass track curved gracefully into a wood whose frosty silence was heightened by a cooing pigeon. After about half a mile the track emerged and then crossed a lane at a point where the site of a signalbox still darkened the grass. A straight sector followed and after that the roofs of a little town. Just short of the town, the track passed what appeared to be a long slab of concrete, covered in weeds. Midway along the slab stood the remains of a booking office, littered with plaster and fallen rafters.

From the town itself came the thunder of lorries and cars shaking the Norman church, cramming the Tudor market place, and unnerving the retired gamekeeper who waited patiently for a gap in the traffic while pneumatic drills crackled beside a hoarding which said "Road Developments. Single Line Traffic." The gamekeeper could remember playing in the middle of that road. Half-consciously, he glanced toward the railway station; and that, too, he could remember, not as a derelict curio but as a thriving necessity and a source of wonder to his grandfather. "If you was to change at Trelawney Junction, my child, you could reach London in six hours. But when I was a lad it took two days, and even then they'd to get out and push the coach up Penmawr Beacon. 'Tis galloping times we'm living in. And they'll be a sight faster when you'm as old as I am."

A description of those vanished railways may sound as though it were written a century ago, yet some of it remained valid within the lifetime of people who are still in their thirties. First, then, comes the clank of a signal at the end of a flower-lined platform, followed soon afterwards by the appearance of a capped and bearded personage who is so much master of the station that he acts as porter and booking clerk also. There are five passengers on the platform: a parson, going to confer at Oxford; a farmer, going to sell at Thame; and three housewives, going to buy at Princes Risborough. Their fellow-travellers include five milk churns, a crate of hens, a packing case (marked *Singapore*), several rolls of barbed wire, two pigs, and a scythe.

Suddenly a distant whistle is heard, a shrill and imperious sound, partly a warning and partly a salutation. Glancing down the line, which sweeps out of sight under a bridge, the passengers see a plume of white smoke, and presently hear a tank engine hauling three coaches, not the anonymous livery of nationalisation, but segments of a rainbow whose spectrum encompasses the whole of Britain—red, blue, brown, green, white—each colour evoking from its henchmen something of the pride which regimental insignia arouse in those who wear them. Although the Great Western may rate itself the lord of all lines, it does not daunt the Great Central fireman nor the Midland shunter. Railwaymen are 'fans' of their own company, and have not yet been taught to regard their employer as a personal enemy.

Louder and louder grows the rhythmic symphony; nearer and nearer floats the billowy cloud. There she comes, rounding the bend; and here at last she is, halted within a yard of the lowered signal. The guard jumps down, the driver wipes his hands on a wisp of cotton waste, the fireman swigs cold tea from a cloudy bottle. The farmer and the housewives embark, but the parson lingers beside the simmering locomotive, oblivious of whatever fantasies are sublimating themselves from Freudian repression. While the guard stows the aforesaid cargo, the station factotum opens a first class compartment for the parson, who happens to be an archdeacon. Accepting a silver threepenny piece, the *ad hoc* porter touches his cap: "Catching the late noight 'ome, Sir?"

K

"Not this time, Thomas. I have to attend a meeting. So it'll be the mid-morning tomorrow."

The porter now strolls up to the engine: "Oi see Fenny Strartford lorst again."

"Oh ah," nods the driver. "Ted Gurney scored a goal against 'isself. Oi 'eard the referee say, 'Are you with 'em or agin 'em?' But oi cheered 'im up arterwards. 'Look at it this way, Ted,' oi said. 'Fenny were seven goals down when it 'appened, so oi don't see as one more would ha' made all thart difference.' "

Returning to his place in the last coach, the guard waves his flag while blowing his whistle, whereupon the driver replies, and the train moves forward, chuff-chuffing through cornfields and pastures where farmfolk look up and sometimes wave, where small boys lean from little bridges, where elderly cottagers exclaim: "Mother! There goes the twelve-fifty. Toime to put the kettle on." Siegfried Sassoon enshrined the sight and sound of every local train:

One hears it disappear
With needless warning whistle and rail-resounding wheels.
"That's quite like an old familiar friend," one feels.

Those branch lines were also lifelines. In the days before cars, they enabled all save the very poor to visit their county town, or a relative twenty miles away, and to return before sunset. In the days before telephones and radio, they were a kind of newspaper, carrying the latest headlines via the London express. Even today they create a local grapevine, circulating rumour and fact.

Meanwhile—still waiting for a gap in the traffic—the patient gamekeeper reflects that Britain's decimated railways are indeed quicker, cleaner, safer, and so much more expensive that they have priced themselves into a permanent mortgage.

II

Signposts to Winter

What is the surest sign that winter has arrived? Not, certainly, a blizzard, for that may occur in spring, and on Ben Nevis its aftermath may linger throughout the year. Temperature, perhaps? But that, too, can mislead, as anyone knows who, having shivered at Ely in April, strolls shirt-sleeved through Fowey in February. Although the sun is an irrefutable timepiece, it will often confound the man who employs it as a calendar. Again, few farmers need to plough in summer, yet many are compelled to plough during the other three seasons. Furrows, therefore, may prove as deceptive as snowflakes and thermometers.

Birds seem to be a better guide. No one in Britain has heard a cuckoo at Christmas nor seen a fieldfare at Whitsun. Yet even the birds exhibit negative behaviour, as, for example, when we say that a magpie seldom whistles in September and that a starling never moults in March. Moreover, the birds are sometimes unseen as well as unheard; and the small mammals likewise. It is true, of course, that mountain hares assume a white camouflage in winter, but they, too, are elusive and by definition not ubiquitous. Trees, on the other hand, *are* ubiquitous, or nearly so; and they remain visible all the year round. Unlike sunshine and snow, which occasionally mock the calendar, a tree abides by the rules, never shedding its leaves in July nor speeding its sap in December. The time of flowering rarely varies by more than a week or two. When the elms are bare we know that October has gone and that May has not yet arrived. Among trees, however, bareness is not a synonym for ungainliness. Shorn sheep are ungainly, but a leafless tree has merely exchanged one type of beauty for another, even as the June greenness is exchanged for an October fieriness.

Few wintry sights are more beautiful than the hilltop trees at early evening, etched against a yellow sky and the last tincture of a scarlet sun. You might almost fancy that the boughs were

twigs, kindling a smokeless fire. When the western sky has faded to the very palest shade of blue, the stars prevail, seeming at one moment to be trinkets on a Christmas tree, and at the next—if a breeze stirs—droplets of quicksilver trickling through the branches. In summertime a tree's strength is overshadowed by its shape, but in winter the sinews stand out, as on Tennyson's oak:

All his leaves
Fallen at length,
Look, he stands
Trunk and bough,
Naked strength.

The ash was called 'Venus of the Woods,' but a woodland code sets strength before beauty, so that precedence belongs to *Quercus robur*, which our forefathers christened 'British Oak'. No other timber looks so well in an old country house, whether as fuel for the hearth or as rafters for the roof. Standing tiptoe at a hundred feet or more, the British oak was both a symbol and a substance of British strength. Admirals scattered scorns on their land, inspired by Garrick's sea shanty:

Heart of oak are our ships,
Jolly tars are our men.

And in those years nobody giggled at the refrain:

We always are ready;
Steady, boys, steady!

Most people look first at a tree's foliage, though its branches are sometimes the surest guide. At any season the willows and Lombardy poplars can be recognised from a distance. Other trees —the silver birch and the wild service, for instance—are easily identified by their bark. Winter uncovers the symmetry of a tree's domestic economy, showing that the longest branches are about the same length as the longest roots. In other words, the leaves drip their moisture where it is most needed, and then, having fallen, spread their compost where it will do most good; an arrangement which the poets have applauded:

And over them, just so,
The dripping branches grow
To slake the yeasty solid
With mineral-tinctured liquid:
So simple, so adroit,
This annual exploit.

"Only God," says the song, "can make a tree." Science prefers to say: "Only a tree can make a tree." No matter how we view it, we must surely marvel at the fact that a tiny embryo in a small seed became one of the yews which have flourished at Fountains Abbey since the Dark Ages. Nor need we feel surprised that our numinous ancestors equated trees with dieties. The laurel was a symbol of Apollo; the vine, of Bacchus; the olive, of Minerva; the myrtle, of Aphrodite. In Britain the deciduous trees wear the battledress of winter, standing like signposts beside rivers, across plains, among valleys. At the end of the day, however, a country-man looks to the hilltop trees, those seemingly changeless pointers through eternal winter, black and bristling and bare; dead trees, insofar as distance reveals neither a leaf nor a bud; battered trees, insofar as they withstand an elemental siege. Yet, within each tree, every one of the millions of cells keeps count of time, silently and sedulously sustaining itself until, like a hibernating creature, it responds to the sun, that solar baton, at whose command the winter's *andante* rises to a spring *crescendo*.

The Man for All Seasons

Six feet tall, blue-eyed and bracken-brown, he looks well in his pink coat and glinting spurs. In theory he retired two years ago, but in practice he still obliges whenever a neighbouring pack is in need of a huntsman. Townsfolk regard him as a Jack-of-all-Trades who spends his summers in idle redundancy, but country-folk see him as an all-the-year-rounder and the master of his craft, which is to lead hounds in hunting their quarry.

Jason began his career by serving as stable lad to a female Master who combined a penchant for beagling with a passion for Bach. Her hounds, in fact, answered to mellifluous names such as Melody, Fugue, Minim, Crotchet, Crescendo. After a spell as second whipper-in with a north country pack, Jason joined the yeomanry as a trooper, and in 1939 sailed with the horses to France, where his steadiness under fire impressed one of the officers. In 1946, therefore, Jason became huntsman with the officer's pack, whence he rose to the summit of his calling, as huntsman in a fashionable shire.

At any time of year a huntsman's day starts early, though never so soon as in September, when cubbing demands a cool and scented start. As the clock strikes five he reaches the kennels. At

half-past five the pack embarks for the meet. Soon after six the
field moves off, and the huntsman's chief task begins. What, then,
are his qualifications for that task? First, he must possess the
innate courtesy and the acquired suavity which enable him to
converse and sometimes to reason with the Master, who may be
a duke, or a farmer, or a colonel, or a spinster. If, like Jason, the
huntsman serves a famous pack, he must know when to say
"My lord" and when not to say "Hold hard, you pot-bellied
tycoon!" Next, he must know more about foxes than the foxes
know, because he will sometimes need to anticipate the tricks of

an old lag that has thrice outwitted the pack. His memory must be a map of the territory, showing every field, covert, earth, bog, stream, road, railway, and tavern. Intent on tracking the fox, he cannot at the same time keep an eye on every member of the pack. That duty belongs to the whipper-in, who may be likened to the Commander in a battleship, responsible for discipline and the day-to-day running of the vessel. Stragglers and squabblers are controlled by the whips, though more effectively than in the House of Commons.

Having risen at four o'clock, the September huntsman may return from cubbing by early afternoon, but his work is not yet done, for he will join the Master at a post-mortem on the day's sport, and will certainly have a word with the stud groom: "Jorrocks has tangled himself on some wire" ... "You were right about Felicity. She'll never make the grade" ... "Her ladyship was the only woman wearing a veil. One of the fillies turned out in yellow jeans."

Winter, however, is the huntsman's most arduous season. Up by 5 a.m., he spends the pitch-black hours preparing for the meet at 11 o'clock. Rain, mist, wind, ice, snow ... mornings when the scent is strong, afternoons when every fox seems to have fled the kingdom ... all these he takes in his stride. When dusk is falling he returns to the kennels, two-thirds asleep; and this he must do every third day of the week.

In spring and summer a huntsman is busy with hounds. Guided by the Master, he allocates the weaned puppies to any follower who has volunteered to 'walk' the youngsters for a year. He hands-over the puppies himself—usually in pairs or 'couples' —and then visits them regularly to ensure they make good progress. About a month after the puppies have been put out to walk, the previous year's puppies return to kennels, ready to learn corporate discipline and the elements of hunting. In cloth cap and white kennel coat the huntsman and his whips stride or cycle many miles a day, exercising their charges.

During the course of his career Jason has learned much about much. He can identify a kestrel before most other people have seen it. One glance at the snow tells him what species of bird or mammal has made the slots thereon. He knows where the rabbits have advanced and why the badgers have retreated. If he is a stag hunter he will assess the stag's age by parsing its antlers.

He can say where a lazy farmer has neglected to harrow his oat-field, and where a bumptious newcomer has erected a fence. The volume of traffic on Saturday, the unofficial closing time on Sunday, the vicar's train-spotting on Monday, the cattle market on Tuesday, the motor rally on Wednesday, the Army manoeuvre on Thursday, the funeral on Friday . . . each is noted by his roving eye, or reported by his ubiquitous grapevine. Like a regional Debrett—and with deeper insight—he can blazon the family backgrounds. He has overheard the whispered endearments between the major and the bailiff's wife. He could scarcely help overhearing the unwhispered unendearments between the earl and the countess. He has seen the braggart shirk a fence, and the coward dare a brook. Psychologically and genealogically he has sifted the tares from the wheat; and in his own temperament he combines canniness with conservatism.

The subject of hunting contrives to bring out the folly of some who approve and of some who disapprove the chase. On the one hand, there are those who affirm that a fox positively enjoys being chased; on the other, there are those who positively affirm that all hunting folk are callous. But the truth is, a fox does *not* enjoy being chased, and the majority of hunting folk are *not* callous. As for the fox, one assumes that it would rather be killed quickly after a chase than die slowly after a pellet wound.

Right or wrong, hunting has long been a feature of country life. It is followed by every section of society and by all age groups from toddlers to dotards; some on foot, some mounted, some in a car. As John Masefield remarked, the music of horse and hound brings Hodge to his feet:

> Then a rattle uphill and a clop downlane
> It emptied the bar of the King of Spain,
> Tom left his cider, Dick left his bitter,
> Granfer James left his pipe and spitter . . .

Scenes from Clerical Life

Life at the Old Rectory has taken-on a new lease since the freehold was acquired by one of Her Majesty's former plenipotentiaries in foreign parts. The new owner seems well-pleased with what he calls 'a real snip'. Perhaps he does not know, or has chosen to forget, that the cost of painting the exterior in 1977 exceeded the cost of building the entire premises in 1707. The house itself includes seven bedrooms, a music gallery (added by a titled incumbent in 1796), stabling for six horses (enlarged by a canon in 1811), together with tennis courts and an acre of garden. During the two centuries of its existence the rectory has witnessed the history of Anglican clergy from their heydays to their present days.

The previous rectory was a medieval cottage, patched-up by any rector who could afford to be parsimonious. Some of the Caroline clergy had no home at all. In 1671, when Viscount Scudamore built a rectory for the homeless priest at Hempsted in Gloucestershire, the second occupant, Archdeacon Gregory, carved a secular *Te Deum* on the doorway:

> Who'er doth dwell within this door
> Thank God for Viscount Scudamore.

The plight of country clergymen went unregarded until 1704, when Queen Anne diverted part of the Crown revenue to create a fund for the relief of ill-housed parsons. The gesture was long overdue because a census had already revealed that more than half the livings in England were worth less than eighty pounds yearly. Some of the curates received less than twelve pounds yearly. The vicar of Goldsmith's "Deserted Village" was therefore lucky as well as lovable:

> A man he was to all the country dear,
> And passing rich on forty pounds a year . . .

Queen Anne's bounty, however, was a palliative, not a cure. Writing of Wiltshire in 1826, William Cobbett remarked: "There are now no less than nine parishes, out of the twenty-nine, that have either no parson-houses, or have such as are in such a state that a parson will not, or cannot, live in them." On the Welsh border the problem was desperate: "More than one-half of the parishes have either no parsonage-houses at all, or have not one that a parson thinks fit for him to live in; and I venture to assert that one or other of these is the case in four parishes out of every five in Herefordshire." At the beginning of the twentieth century the country clergy were still saddled with tumbledown houses and inequitable stipends. Thus, while one vicar received £3,000 yearly and a modest house, his neighbouring colleague received a stipend that hardly met the cost of maintaining his twelve-room parsonage. The Church Commissioners ultimately abolished many of the injustices, but some of them survived into recent times. During the 1930s, for example, Radstock Rectory in Somerset possessed neither a bathroom nor a fitted wash basin, while at Beeston in Nottinghamshire the rector's wife had to walk fifteen yards from her kitchen to the nearest water tap. In 1955 the bathroom at Charlecombe Rectory in Somerset was an attic containing a twenty-gallon oil drum over a paraffin stove that heated water which had been carried upstairs in buckets. In 1957 the rector of Saint Mary's at Rye in Sussex occupied one room in the wall of his church.

Among the handful of clergy who could afford to build their own home was Sidney Smith, who in 1806 became rector of the Yorkshire parish of Foston le Clay, where the parsonage was (as he put it) 'a hovel'. Smith therefore designed a new rectory, employing a mason and a carpenter to help him with the building. "I live," he wrote, "trowel in hand, and my whole soul is filled with lath and plaster." The cost of the house, its roads, and the adjacent farm buildings was about £3,950. Boasting that his new home was "the equal of any inn on the North Road," Smith called it 'The Rector's Head'.

Like the oldest man in the world, the oldest parsonage in the kingdom is a subject of debate. Among the undoubted veterans is the twelfth-century Priest's House at Alfriston in Sussex, the first property ever to be bought by the National Trust. Men of Kent, on the other hand, may support Kentish Men in protesting that the Alfriston house seems a mere stripling when compared with the Canterbury house which lodged Saint Augustine and his monks more than 1,300 years ago. Meanwhile, former parsonages change hands at prices exceeding the lifelong stipends of their Victorian incumbents. In Sussex the Tudor parsonage at Northiam was recently valued at £44,000. Three Dorset parsonages were offered for sale at prices ranging from £32,000 to £50,000. Some of our 'progressive' priests, by contrast, believe that the clergy ought to follow a famous non-property owning precept: "The Son of Man hath not where to lay his head." One or two—indeed, three or four—deans and bishops appear to feel guilty because their predecessors were housed in a manner reflecting the spirit of the age and the influence of the Church. Such men, one feels, would, if they could, demolish Saint Paul's Cathedral and then sell the rubble in order to buy guns for 'freedom fighters'.

England's country parsonages recall an era that has passed away forever. Many villages nowadays possess no resident priest; many villagers never enter a church unless to be baptised, married, or buried. Yet those parsonages compile a resounding *Who's Who* ... Robert Herrick of Dean Prior in Devonshire, Sabine Baring-Gould of Lew Trenchard in the same county, Gilbert White of Selborne in Hampshire, Charles Kingsley of Eversley in the same county, George Herbert of Fugglestone Saint Peter in Wiltshire, George Crabbe of Aldeburgh in Suffolk, John Wyclif of Lutterworth in Leicestershire, R. S. Hawker of Morwenstow in Cornwall, John Henry Newman of Littlemore in Oxfordshire, William Barnes of Winterbourne Came in Dorset, Horatio Nelson (son of the rector of Burnham Thorpe in Norfolk), Alfred Tennyson (son of the rector of Somersby in Lincolnshire), Ralph Vaughan Williams (son of the vicar of Down Ampney in Gloucestershire), and (pater-familias extraordinary) Patrick Brontë of Haworth in Yorkshire.

A Few Days in Bed

I lately received news of an old friend whom I call the Chiltern hermit, though 'hermit' must not be mistaken for 'misanthrope', because—as well as being visited by a niece and her family—the old chap goes the rounds of cronies in the village. All the same, he does live alone in a remote cottage atop a steep hill, and he does suffer certain minor infirmities which have underlined his own topographical remark: "It's all 'ills 'ere."

Anyway, at the very moment when I was beginning to wonder whether no news really is good news, I received a letter from a mutual acquaintance, which may be enlarged as follows: not long ago the vicar called at the hermit's cottage, and was surprised to find a message pinned on the front door, saying *Back Tuesday*.

Since it is well-known that the hermit last left the Chilterns in 1936, and since he returned thither after twelve hours, utterly disillusioned by a sponsored visit to the House of Commons . . . these things being so, the vicar was, as I say, surprised by the brief and cryptic message.

His surprise turned to anxiety when neither the postman nor the policeman could say whither the hermit had gone, nor why. Being a good shepherd, the vicar went in search of his lost and occasionally conforming lamb, whom he finally traced to a hospital. Without waiting to make further inquiries, the vicar drove at once to see his parishioner, fearing the worst, and at best expecting to find him bed-ridden in a geriatric ward. You may therefore imagine the vicar's astonishment on being taken to a small private room, where he found the patient in excellent spirits, leaning against an armchair while smoking the sort of tobacco that would have killed lesser men before their fiftieth birthday.

"Oi aren't agoing to die," the patient declared. "Oi'm just 'ere for my 'ealth."

The vicar glanced at the nurse, who was more explicit. "It's only a varicose vein," she said. "Everything went well, and tomorrow or the next day he'll be home again." And with that cheerful prognosis the girl departed.

"You," said the hermit, "was expecting to see me in a public ward." He was so right that his visitor could only nod. "Instead of which, oi'm one o' those queue-crashing capitalists as is causing the under-privileged to die for lack of medical attention."

The vicar was still perplexed. "It's loike this," the hermit explained. "Oi value my privacy. Oi always 'ave done, ever since my auntie took to growing roses round the garden toilet. 'One o' these days,' oi said to myself, 'you're going to need a hoperation, and you won't loike it when they take your teeth out in front of all them other patients. So,' oi said, 'you'd better do something about it'."

"You mean . . ."

"Oi mean oi put summat by each month. Not much, moind, 'cause oi never 'ad much. But enough to give me a bit o' privacy for a week or two. Near thirty year oi've been paying out, and now oi'm gitting a bit o' my own back." He lowered his voice, as though aware that he was about to speak very frankly. "Oi'll tell you summat, vicar. All this noice room and all them noice nurses they 'aven't cost me no more a month nor wart some silly bastards gives away to the brewers on a Sartdee noight."

"Well, well, well," the vicar exclaimed, lost in amazement and admiration.

"Was thart a sin?"

"Some people would say . . ."

"Oi know wart some people would say. Oi've 'eard it down The Wheatsheaf. 'Eard it from charps as take 'ome sixty quid a week, which is three toimes more'n oi ever earned in a fort-noight. Anyow, the surgeon wart cut me up . . . he wasn't a doctor . . . he were a plain mister . . . still, he seemed to know wart he were doing . . . anyow, he fair laughed when oi said 'Oi 'ope you're sure there's no poor soul as is suffering on account of oi put a bit by each month'. And do you know wart he said?"

"Well?"

" 'Friend,' he said, 'even if you was the King of England,' he said, 'thart still wouldn't stop me from tending someone whose need was greater than your own. Oi only wish,' he said, 'as certain bloody fools would git thart simple truth into their thick 'eads.' A very outspoken gentleman is Mr Smith."

"So it appears."

"Ah, and when he come to see me after the hoperation he said, 'Gawd dammit,' he said, 'you're a tough old bird'."

"Then let us thank heaven for it," murmured the vicar.

"Strictly speaking," the hermit continued, "my subscription would keep me 'ere for quoite a toime." He glanced at the gay curtains, the bowl of flowers, the kind message. "Between you and me, vicar, oi've 'alf a moind to suffer a relapse."

"Not . . ."

"Not long, moind. Just another couple of days. Thart'd save me going down to collect the milk."

"But why was all this kept so secret?"

"It's loike wart oi said . . . if them Labour charps ever got to know as oi'd put by a bit each month they'd start calling me a Fascist pig. Thart's the state we're in nowadays. Even in the countrysoide."

The vicar, a practising non-politician, refrained from comment. After a cup of tea, however, the two men stood with bowed heads, and one of them was silent while the other gave thanks to the wonders of science, and the dedication of doctors and nurses, and the justice of a system that allows a tough old bird to put by a bit each month and so acquire the privacy which many richer people rate as less valuable than drinking and gambling and smoking.

12

The Lady with a Lamp

The young man stood knee-deep in snow, unaware that he was shivering. Behind him the farmhouse window shone like an orange in the night. Suddenly he blinked. Then he shouted: "Is that Nurse?"

A distant lantern seemed to answer: "Aye, 'tis Nurse."

"How in God's name did'st get here?"

"Dost not know? I'm an angel. I've wings."

"But to travel alone . . ."

"Who said I was alone? Angel or not, I've brought a boy-friend."

But we must go back several hours. In fact, we must go back seventy years, to a December evening when the Yorkshire grapevine reported: "T'lass at Fell Farm is nigh mothering. They say young Garth is fair frantic. The doctor's ill, and the shepherd took an hour to cover a mile. Looks like we mun find Tom."

Tom was the farrier, a sure and skilful rock in any crisis. So, while the district nurse warmed her hands at the smithy fire, Tom fixed some metal runners to a sledge. "Happen thee and me mun play Santa Claus," he muttered. "There's nowt else possible in this weather." That settled, he harnessed his own horse, and away they went, over the frozen beck, up to the snowbound fells.

Thus it came to pass that the nurse was able to reach her patient, leaving Tom to sip cocoa in the kitchen while the young husband paced anxiously up and down. The farrier glanced at the snow still thawing from his waist downward. "It were a cool journey," he admitted.

L

Garth swung round. "But how were we to know she'd be afore her time, and th'owd doctor took queer, and the snow six foot deep, and the nearest telephone wi' its wires down, and the sheep smothered, and feyther poorly, and mother stranded way beyond Biggins, and . . ." The young man gave up the unequal struggle.

Himself the father of four children, Tom laid a paternal hand on Garth's shoulder. "Look, lad," he said, "this sort o' caper is as old as Eden. And dammit some o' the lasses survived. Aye, and some o' the babes, too." As though by way of confirmation, a pair of very young lungs suddenly announced that a man-child had entered the world, and that in due course the government of Fell Farm would be upon his shoulder.

Three hours later, Tom and Nurse re-entered the smithy, cold but content. Like Juliet's nurse, they might well have exclaimed: "I am a-weary . . . how my bones ache! What a jaunt I have had!" But Nurse only remarked: "Next time happen they'll arrange things more seasonably. July's a nice month for climbing yon fell."

That tradition of service has not died with the years. One north country nurse—now serving the district which her own mother used to serve—often receives a genealogical welcome, as when an elderly woman whispers: "Thy mother brought my youngest in't world, so maybe 'tis right thou should'st see me out of it." Lapsing deliberately into a dying dialect, the nurse replies with kindly no-nonsense: "Thee's nobbut a silly owd woman. I keep telling thee, it is *not* a heart attack. It isn't even bronchitis. It's a simple case of bellyache, brought on by all that tatie pie in't village hall last night. Mother warned thee agin a second helping, but thou wouldn't listen, and this is the result. So for once in a while thee'll have to take thy medicine lying down."

It is as well that some women do not share Richard Jefferies' horror of illness. "Human suffering," he declared, "is so great, so endless, so awful that I can hardly bear to write of it. I could not go into hospital and face it, as some do, lest my mind should be temporarily overcome." In nurses, by contrast, love casts out not only fear but also revulsion and all uncharitableness; nor could it be otherwise, for it was love that dedicated them to a standard of living which is basically a standard of giving. Bearing a burden that might otherwise fall to our over-strained hospitals, the district nurse carries loving-kindness to the highest hill of

fear and to the darkest valley of death. In the words of the
Prayer Book, she "looks down in pity and compassion on this
thy afflicted servant." Disregarding whatever anxieties may be
afflicting her own life, she listens patiently, works gently, and
instructs firmly. Fortunately, the nurse's burden is nowadays
lightened by equipment and expertise which in her mother's
youth did not exist and could scarcely be imaged . . . instead of a
sledge, an ambulance; instead of a bicycle, a car; instead of a
prayer, a drug.

These kind and capable women represent our last link with the
old psycho-somatic rapport between a doctor and his patient.
They know all about Grannie's sister in New Zealand, and the
son whose picture is turned to the wall. Again like Juliet's nurse,
they may have known their patient in the years "when 'twas a
little prating thing". To the bed-ridden they bring news of the
world. To the convalescent they seem more important than the
dawn itself: "He thinks," Lamb confessed, "only of the regular
return of the same phenomenon at the same hour tomorrow."

Symptoms are indeed treated more efficaciously than ever
before, and in an ever-increasing number of patients, which is
one reason why the patients themselves are sometimes treated in
ways which an old-fashioned doctor would have regarded as
impersonal and therefore harmful. Science is still embarrassed by
the invalid who says: "Nay, lass, t'wasn't thy medicine. I poured
the filthy stuff down't drain. What got *me* up and about was the
nice long chat we had yesterday." Could any general practitioner
now practise that kind of therapy?

Few people ever have served mankind without counting the
cost to their own store of worldly wealth. Among them are the
nurses who drive through a midnight blizzard, or keep watch
in a children's ward, bringing health to many, and comfort to all.

Christmas Decorations

The wild days that we call grey offer an acceptable challenge. The
mild days that we call grey offer a quiet charm. And both the
charm and the challenge spring partly from the fact that those days
are not grey at all, or, rather, are not all grey. If by 'days' we mean
the sights that are visible between dawn and dusk, then even the

greyest days are many-coloured because winter's greyness appears chiefly in the sky whence it enhances whatever it not grey.

In summer and autumn the flowers and the trees and the crops are so steeped in sunshine that their richness becomes an embarrassment. Like beggars at a banquet, we scarcely know where to begin, and are forever flitting from one dish to another, as though the next might prove more delicious than the last. December makes no such demands. When a ploughed field catches the eye, it does so because the clouds have heightened its russet sobriety. When a mountain beck catches the eye, it does so because the clouds have enhanced its foaming eddies. The same is true of the trees which, although they are dressed in black, do not mourn the loss of summer's finery, for they have grown old gracefully, and grace is grace throughout the year.

If we study a grey sky we may decide that the greyness is an optical illusion, caused not by defective vision but by our own laziness, which tends to slap the label 'grey' on to objects which could more properly be described as 'blue-grey'. Certainly we ought not to assume that greyness is always a synonym for melancholy. If, for example, we receive bad news we regard a sunless day as though it were a fellow-sufferer. If, on the other hand, we receive good news we either disregard the weather or accept it as a man accepts the rain while he sits by his own fireside. The rain, in short, deepens his inner comfort even as the dark months kindled Emily Brontë's inner light:

> I shall smile when wreaths of snow
> Blossom where the rose should grow;
> I shall sing when night's decay
> Ushers in the drearier day.

What of the days that really are dreary? The days when the sun rises and sets unseen, when the rain falls like perpetual motion, when even the snow loses something of its brightness to a low and scowling sky? The first thing to be said about such days is, they are rare; the second thing is, they reward any seeker who explores the nuances of a chiaroscuro. Is there not a blurred beauty in firelit windows flickering through fog? Or in signposts that loom six feet away, pointing prophetically to an invisible destination?

Meanwhile, a cursory glance through this window suggests

that Advent has produced yet another day of grey skies, withered flowers, leafless trees. A second and more searching glance reveals that some of the clouds are edged with silver linings which cannot wholly hide the blue beneath them. As for the withered flowers, they are indeed on show in places where the gardener has not pruned or uprooted them. But the chrysanthemums flourish alongside a few hardy dahlias and one rosebush heavy with buds. The customary primrose is in bloom, conspicuous as a guest who has arrived too soon. All the old familiar faces are there—marigolds, pansies, antirrhinums, sweet williams—each bereaved of most of its contemporaries, yet none failing to make the best of a gentle western climate.

Holly berries gleam like little wintry suns warming the beech hedges that stretch like strips of copper with a hint of ginger in them. When the breeze stirs, their leaves utter a sound midway between a swish and a crinkle. When one of them falls, it strikes the ground with a pointed edge, after the manner of a tiptoe ballet dancer. And when the breeze becomes a gust, the leaf trips away as merrily as though its funeral were a wedding. Then there are the scarlet hips and haws, the puddles of sodden straw, the lividly unedible fungi, the tips of snowdrops and anemones peering through a patch of soil that has been eroded by rain.

Sparkling like pale palms, the wayside ferns justify Leigh Hunt's paradox: "Christmas is a kind of spring." Above them droop the last of the lemon-tinted hazel leaves and the black-berry's rusty ochre. Bright-eyed and head-cocked at the kitchen door, a robin flaunts his cheerful chest-protector while finches flash like emerald shadows among black branches. It seems only the other day that the farmer was sowing oats, but now the crop outshines the grass.

On the hill a flock of white sheep wear a daub of red dye that glows like a rear light. Below the hill, smoke from the farmhouse chimney climbs in a straight line and then, meeting the breeze, becomes a question mark chasing its own tail. By mid-afternoon the first lamplit window winks and then stares steadily, dimming all the other colours. If you delve more deeply you will discover not only that every object is coloured but also that every object is a series of colours, as in the grass (whose stems look almost white) and in the lichened trees (where silver and olive are set against orange and purple). Delving even deeper, you unearth the wormlike skeins that will pave the woods with Maytime blue-bells. Deeper still, the bulbs and corms are neither dead nor sleeping, but alive and wide-awake.

So there they are, the colours which we too often classify as grey. Admittedly, they do not dazzle the eye. On the contrary, they seem sometimes to elude it. Neither their quality nor their quantity can challenge the pageants that confirm the spring, and announce the summer, and bury the autumn. Nevertheless, December's decorations do appear, seldom startling, often surprising, always a source of pleasure.

Of Cabbages and Kings

Having lived and died more or less unknown, Mary Webb, the Shropshire writer, was made famous, literally overnight, by a speech that was delivered to the Royal Literary Fund by the prime minister, Stanley Baldwin. Mary Webb's poetry and prose, he said, were shamefully neglected. While literary cliques regarded life beyond the London postal district as no longer significant, Baldwin carried the fight into the Philistines' camp. "The stupid urban view of the countryside as dull," he declared, "receives a fresh and crushing answer in the books of Mary Webb." Baldwin's own experience saved him from spoiling a good case by overstating it, else he might have insisted that country life is at all times and in every way as dramatic as town life. But a countryman knows that affairs of State and matters of fashion are decided by a relatively small number of people in London. Unless he has an entrée to those circles he must take his information from newspapers and broadcasts.

Politicians, however, still forgather at country houses, and to that extent a few privileged rustics take their information straight from the horse's mouth or at any rate from the lips of a reliable groom. This kind of news sometimes reaches the middle-aged bachelor who occupies a cottage on his elder brother's estate, and is known locally as Mr Edwards, a man steeped in many aspects of country life, from fox hunting and ornithology to parish boundaries and family histories. Mr Edward spends most of his time on the estate, partly because he prefers to do so and partly because his income is small. Like Blake, he can find eternity not perhaps in a grain of sand, but certainly in six hundred acres of mixed farming. The elder brother, by contrast, counts among his friends a number of politicians and writers, for whom he gives an occasional house party, attended by Mr Edward, who feels somewhat adrift in such an urbanely urban society. The conversation, however, fascinates him. "Maggie Thatcher told me ..." ... "Jim, I said, you're not the first PM whose supporters don't support him" ... "I gather that the Palace took a very dim view" ... "He's in a tricky position. His majority is less than safe, and most of his constituents are very Left, so if they ever do get to know how many shares he holds ..."

Not, himself, a bookish man—and the reverse of a spiteful one—Mr Edward is frequently pained by the remarks of best-selling novelists and subsidised poets. "I've just finished his new book. Three hundred pages. The first four paragraphs are excellent" ... "He ruined his chances by saying he admired Bridges's poems. But Sally was more astute. She just said, 'What *are* Bridges?'" ... "They turned it down at first, but then somebody had the bright idea of adding a Lesbian interest, and now the thing's being paperbacked."

From his corner behind the piano Mr Edward sees a cabinet minister in the flesh. He watches an unmarried playwright glance at himself in the mirror. He observes a life peer looking for the hallmark on a spoon. He notices a Dame easing her shoe. He hears once again the snippets of conversation: "When I last met Kissinger ..." ... "It'll all go according to plan. They'll strike, and when they've almost ruined the firm they'll return to work. Then the Treasury will fork out a few millions, and the firm will be more or less nationalised" ... "He's really out for a peerage, but his PPS admits he'd be willing to vote nicely in exchange for a knighthood" ... "Take it from me, the Bill won't even be drafted."

How remote it all seems from Mr Edward's world, his early rising to watch the stags, his noonday talk with the roadmender, his late-night study of the badgers, his general concern for the state of the world as it affects Hillcrest Farm and Ashby-juxta-Pontem. He finds it strange that the cabinet minister and the Arts Council poet should pay no attention to this year's haycrop in Parson's Piece nor to next year's cabbages in Five Acres. And he still remembers the previous house party, when the Taxmaster-

General, having been conducted round the stables, said to his host: "Good God, Tony, that brother of yours has nearly walked me off my feet." In fact, the long day's march covered about two-thirds of a mile.

Meanwhile, having sipped a sherry and nodded a greeting, Mr Edward walks unobtrusively on to the terrace and thence to the moonlit stream and its cargo of stars. Above the silence, he hears a breeze in the aspen, and a fox in the covert, and—from the far side of the hill—young Perkins on his motor cycle, returning from The Wheatsheaf. Never one to strain after originality, he murmurs: "It takes all sorts to make a world. Somebody's got to govern. Somebody's got to be the custodians' custodian. But personally . . ." and here he addresses the stream, "personally, I'd pay twenty thousand a year *not* to sit in Number Ten."

Presently he rejoins the party, listening rather than talking. "They say his next play contains no dialogue at all. I hope to God they're right" . . . "It's not the Lords that ought to be abolished. It's the electorate" . . . "His union voted him a Rolls-Royce, but he attends branch meetings on a bicycle" . . . "She didn't realise they were still on the air, so she turned round to chancellor and shouted, 'Despite what we've all been saying, I still think our policy is absolutely disastrous'."

As soon as he decently can, Mr Edward takes leave of his host and hostess, adding: "By the way, Tony, I'll be knocking-up some new gateposts tomorrow." At the servants' entrance he steps into his gumboots, pausing for a word with the stockman, who on these occasions is disguised as plain clothes footman. "George, next time you pass Hillcrest, take a look at those elms. I think they've had it."

Across three silent fields, past a rustling wood, over a timber bridge, and there glow his own lamplit curtains. Hearing him, the spaniels utter a welcome. For the first time since he knotted his bow tie, Mr Edward feels at ease. Half an hour later, leaning from the bedroom window, he can just glimpse the lights at the Hall. Then, with an enigmatic "Thank God," he adjusts the reading lamp, and settles down to *Memoirs of an MFH*.

Elegy for a Tree

When Browning's exile pined for England in April, what was the feature of the scene which first came to his mind? A cuckoo? A daffodil? A primrose? Did he remember that the lambs were frisking, the blossom was snowing, the sun was shining? No, he remembered

> That the lowest boughs and the brush-wood leaf
> Round the elm-tree bole are in tiny leaf . . .

A Tudor botanist, John Goodyer, kept a watchful eye on the elm's progress. "Before the leaves come forthe," he wrote, "the flowers appear, about the end of March, which grow on the twigs or branches closely compacted or thrust together . . . after which come the first seed . . ." The middle-sized leaves, he added, "are two inches broad, and three inches long, some are longer and broader, some narrower or shorter, rough or harsh in handling on both sides, nickt or indented about the edges . . . This Elme is common to all parts of England where I have travelled." Britain contains several members of the *Ulmaceae* family. The best-known species is the common elm or *Ulmus procera*, a tall tree with tiers of spreading branches whose flowers create a reddish haze during early spring. Unlike the common elm, which was introduced by the Romans, the wych elm or *Ulmus glabra* is a native, sometimes called Scots elm, though it flourishes in many parts of England.

Like good health, a tree is taken for granted until we lose it. Britain, alas, has lost millions of elms during the past decade, victims of a disease carried by bark beetles. Fifty years ago, if an afflicted branch were lopped and burned, the tree had a fair chance of remaining sound, but the epidemic has become so virulent that nothing seems able to cure it. Perhaps that is why the elm tree at last receives an overdue re-appraisal. Many poets have saluted the oak, the ash, the poplar, the lime. Many have saluted cedars, birches, chestnuts, willows, pines. Even the gnarled thorn receives a paean. But you must search hard in order to find the elm's eulogy. Spenser's "vine-proppe elme" may live for centuries; it may also decay and become hollow long

before that time; wherefore Kipling warned us "the Ellum hateth mankind," and is liable

> To drop a limb on the head of him
> Who anyway trusts her shade."

Aldous Huxley was less timid. Indeed, the elm inspired him to try his hand at poetry:

The tiny leaves of April's earliest growing
Powder the tree—so vaporously light
They seem to float, billows of emerald foam . . .

In summer the leaves create both a sunshade and a nightcap, as Milton observed:

Under the shady roof
Of branching elm star-proof.

Tennyson looked with affection on the elms at Somersby Rectory in Lincolnshire:

The seven elms and poplars four
That stand beside my father's door.

Although elm cannot vie with oak and ash as a fuel for the hearth, it remained popular as a source of domestic furniture until the eighteenth century, when merchants began to import exotic timber from distant lands. Yet a well-seasoned elm has its merits. During the 1930s Walter Rose, a carpenter at Haddenham in Buckinghamshire, declared that the tree "served many useful purposes, especially for farm work where strength was required . . . My father always kept a stock of English elm ready sawn and seasoned . . . the two inch plank was used for making dough troughs for bakers, and the solid wheels of sheep troughs." Nor was the elm reserved solely for the simpler kinds of craftsmanship. "I have seen," said Rose, "the tops of refectory tables made of it to which age and polish had given a deep bloom, as of a ripe plum." During the 1940s a few Chiltern bodgers were still making beechwood Windsor chairs, using elm for the seat. A set of 'country Hepplewhite' chairs is nowadays a valuable asset, perfectly at home in a small country house. An elm floor, too, can be made to shine as sleekly as an oak (these words are being written in a study whose floor is partly of elm and partly of oak, each responding equally to years of frequent polishing).

Nowhere do the elms stand more stately than beside the green lanes of Warwickshire and among the meadows which Shakespeare knew, and Michael Drayton also, another Warwickshire poet, who wrote of

Those trees whose bodies seemed by their so massy weight
To press the solid earth, and with their wondrous height
To climb into the clouds . . .

Set singly, or in twos and threes, they rise like timber islets from a green ocean, so invitingly cool in summer that only chronic anxiety will cause a countryman to shun the shelter of their boughs. Sauntering near Stratford-upon-Avon, Ruskin admired "the shadowy groups and lines of elms". Perhaps the cottagers still chant the old Warwickshire jingle:

> When elm leaves are as big as a penny,
> You must plant kidney beans if you mean to have any.

Since rabbits have survived myxomatosis, may not elms one day withstand the plague that has laid so many of them low? At least we can hope that science will find a remedy. Meanwhile, the loss of these handsome trees may with some reservations be likened to a famous Biblical bereavement: "Rachel weeping for her children, and would not be comforted because they are not."

On the Stroke of Midnight

When the clock struck midnight the ghillie rose to his feet. Glancing round at the festive company, he linked hands with the doctor and the dominie. Then, as the twelfth chime died away, he led the New Year salutations:

> Should auld acquaintance be forgot,
> And never brought to min'?

While the song unfolded, the singers became conscious that they were members of a choir which at that very moment was singing those very words throughout Britain, literally from Land's End to John o'Groats. If a singer had relatives in Russia or in Canada or Africa, he knew that there also, at the appropriate hour, the same question would be asked and by implication answered:

> Should auld acquaintance be forgot,
> And days o' lang syne?

An hour later the last of the company stepped unsteadily into his car. Having advanced six yards, and reversed six yards, he fell asleep over the wheel. Awakened by the cold at four a.m., he took a brisk stroll down the village street and then drove home, where, in lieu of breakfast, he ate the cheese and pickles which his wife prepared during the previous evening. "This time," she had insisted, "I shall expect you home soon after midnight." This time, however—as at most other similar times—the reveller offered the same excuse: "I was a wee dram late."

Christmas in the Scottish countryside is overshadowed by the New Year or Hogmanay, from the Norman-French *Hoguinane*, an ancient and not always seemly celebration. The English, for their part, are often puzzled to understand why Scotland regards the birth of a year as more momentous than the birth of a Saviour. Until quite recent times—when the festival became largely pagan—the Scots rated Christmas Day as a working day, unless it fell on a Sunday, and even then the Dickensian spirit was tepid. Why? The best answer came from a Presbyterian minister who, when Christmas did fall on a Sunday, conducted the service without referring to the Nativity. On being asked to justify his omission, the Calvinist replied: "I dinna' hold wi' carols and candles. A Christian should leave such baubles to the Bishop o' Rome." A comparable attitude was imposed on the English by Cromwell and his republican saints who not only banned the Prayer Book but also abolished Christmas and its cheerful festivities. John Evelyn, for example, was arrested because he went to church on Christmas morning; a Sussex washerwoman was whipped because she sang carols on Christmas Eve; and a Worcestershire squire was fined because "he did give to 12 poore men a Christmas dinner and pies." As if to emphasise that plum pudding was ungodly, the House of Commons sat throughout Christmas week.

Unlike the Roundheads, Robert Burns showed little interest in theology. His modest contribution to divine worship, entitled *A New Psalm for the Chapel at Kilmarnock*, is simply a paean for the King's recovery of health. Given an ample supply of liquor and lassies, the Bard of Alloway would have been content either to disregard Christmas or to celebrate it on Midsummer Night. His famous song, however, has become an international anthem. Wherever two or three Scotsmen are gathered together on New Year's Eve, there you will find whisky and Burns, even although the revellers have forgotten the meaning of *drumlie*, and never did know the meaning of *lee-lang*. To the braw lads of the Scottish Border the anniversary of Burns' birthday in January seems more important than the Feast of Saint Andrew in November; and not only to the Scots, because the cult has spread among the English borderers who at Wooler hold their own Burns' Night, toasting 'the immortal memory' of the man whose New Year hymn is chanted by prisoners in jail, by sailors at sea, by strangers on railway stations. It is the fault of the singers, not of the song, that the camaraderie so swiftly fades. Without those December chimes and those January stanzas the mood might fade into an even deeper oblivion.

When Hogmanay is kept as a secular spree it gives rise to drunkenness, but when it is kept as a family festival, or as a communion of thoughtful friends, it may transcend all differences of age and class and creed, inviting a Moslem immigrant to join hands with a Highland atheist who in turn reaches out for Roman Catholics and Zion Baptists. So, the Ayrshire ploughboy's poem has spread throughout the kingdom and thence to many places overseas. Scarcely less remarkable is the timing of his achievement, for, as Stevenson observed, "He composed in six winter months the bulk of his more important poems." What a lesson for our own poets, or at any rate for those who seek to stir the hearts of ordinary men and women.

Walking down a midnight lane on New Year's Eve, many a traveller has been cheered and also chastened by a lamplit window showing three generations ready to raise their glasses and to sing Scotland's song. Time has not yet eradicated the immemorial emotions which rise when the self-propagating year utters a wordless *Salve et Ave*, for then we are aware that our feeble antennae can detect only a fraction of the cosmic vastness, only a tick of the quartz clock, and nothing at all of their ultimate significance. Man appears to be the only terrestrial creature who analyses his predicament, as millions of Britons will be doing on New Year's Eve while with courage and hope they pledge their fellow-pilgrims in words whose simplicity makes the whole world kin:

> For auld lang syne, my dear,
> For auld lang syne,
> We'll tak a cup o' kindness yet,
> For auld lang syne.